LIVING IN JOY

LIVING IN JOY

CREATING POSITIVE CHANGE ONE SMALL GLORIOUS STEP AT A TIME

NOREEN KELTY WITH MICHAEL J. CARLOS

Endorsements

"From her early years of unexpectedly losing her father to being a single mother to her diagnosis of MS, Noreen Kelty is a fighter, a survivor and truly someone who knows how to change a negative situation into a growth opportunity. One of her mottos is 'Small steps and positive self-talk,' and she shows us how that idea can transform our lives. Noreen reminds us with the many insightful and colorful stories of her life how we always have a choice in how we will perceive a situation. With exercises, humor, and vulnerability, Noreen sets the example of how we can move through any of our issues with the grace, wisdom, and humor that she so beautifully models through her stories. Noreen Kelty proves that if you take success principals and really apply them to your life, your life will change for the better. A must read for anyone on a healing and spiritual path!"

Karen Drucker

Singer, Songwriter, Speaker and Author of *Let Go of the Shore*

***

"I cried at least three times reading this heartfelt memoir of love and grit. I have known Noreen for a decade; I am delighted she has put her life down in writing so that others can be inspired and helped on their path. Noreen's indomitable spirit packs a punch and she lives The Success Principles to the nth degree. This book, *Living in Joy*, will inspire you and remind you to be grateful, and to look for the lessons life is giving you. How many times have I heard Noreen's reminders (in her unmistakable New Yawk accent), whispering in my ear, even if a continent away), 'Megha: the Universe is conspiring for your highest good.' It is clear from reading this book that neither Diabetes, nor MS, nor anything else will ever get Noreen down. We are blessed to know Noreen; the world is now blessed to have this book. By the end of this book Noreen in all her glory is standing jubilant and happy with a clear message 'CHOOSE JOY.' Here's to *Living in Joy*!

Megha Nancy Buttenheim

CJO (Chief JOY Officer) and Founding Director: Let Your Yoga Dance® LLC, 35 year faculty: Kripalu Center

***

"If you ever met Noreen Kelty, you know she is a FORCE OF NATURE. And now, in her book, we get an intimate look as to how she became the joyous teacher she is. Noreen isn't a 'talking head' or a removed guru. She is speaking from the trenches and from her big heart. Get ready, because her gusto for life might just open your heart."

Tama Kieves

USA Today featured career catalyst and author of *Thriving Through Uncertainty: Moving Beyond Fear of the Unknown and Making Change Work for You* and more

***

"Noreen Kelty's enthusiasm and passion is not only inspiring, but also contagious. She has a positive attitude and real sense of joy. In this book she honestly shares some of her pain and struggles and the lessons she learned and uses them to teach you how to create positive change. Noreen has been part of the Canfield community since 2010. I love her for her generous heart, fun loving spirit, authenticity, service, gratitude and dedication to the Mirror Exercise. This book will inspire and empower."

Patty Aubery

Co-Founder, The Canfield Training Group

4

Acknowledgements

I am thankful for all the friends I have met along the way.

***

Special thanks to all my clients who encouraged me and supported my business in the early days of "You Bring Me Joy."

***

To Norma Mosia, whose kind heart and willingness to listen had quite an impact on me as a child.

***

To Maggie Jerchau, for making losing weight so much fun and encouraging me as a Weight Watchers Leader.

***

To Patty Anglin, who gave me a BELIEVE stone the day before Weight Watchers Basic Leader Skills training and who always believed in me.

***

To Susan Zirilli, my Weight Watchers mentor, who believed I was capable of great things.

***

To Jeff Bittner, for designing my book cover.

***

To Patty Aubery, for her generosity of spirit and for gifting me a makeover in February 2016.

***

To Carmela Ragusa, who attended, supported, and sometimes assisted me with so many of my business and life adventures.

***

To Patty Prifti Mathis, my walking partner from 2002-2016, we talked and walked many steps while creating so many positive changes.

***

To Joann Ryan, who walked the path at the same time as me as we went through the process of divorce, having someone who understood was so comforting.

***

To Joanne Paternoster and Jeannette Roe, two of my earliest clients who cheered me on at "You Bring Me Joy" and "Joyfilled Lifestyle" and went on to become dear friends who have been at my side through ups and downs.

***

To Jurian Hughes, from Yoga Teacher Training, who discovered I was a reverse breather leading to some important realizations and has supported me through many events.

***

To Tama Kieves, for unleashing my calling and giving me the profound quote: "You can deny your heart or deny your limits."

***

To Jesse Ianniello Mann, whose kindness encouraged me to attend my first Breakthrough to Success in 2011. Her supportive friendship ever since has been a gift.

***

To Jack Canfield, for The Success Principles, his kindness, his encouragement, his friendship and his mentoring which has dramatically changed my life for the better.

***

To Theresa Davis, my accountability partner since 2011, who inspired me to start the mirror exercise and get up early each morning to share our intentions for the day and has been by my side for all business and life trials and triumphs ever since.

***

To Megha Nancy Buttenheim, who has shared the Dance of Joy with me so many times in so many ways.

***

To my former husband, Mike Carlos, for sharing this amazing experience of parenting Kelly and Michael and for his tremendous support after the MS diagnosis.

***

To Janice Driscoll, for many years practicing yoga on and off the mat, for supporting me through all the trials and triumphs, who taught me there is room for it all and the true meaning of compassion without judgement using two words-So What??!!

***

To Karen Drucker, who has soothed my soul, lifted my spirits and healed my heart more times than I can count, I am so blessed by our friendship.

***

To Patti Kelty Renart, my sister, my friend, for always making me feel so loved, admired and appreciated and making me laugh harder than anyone else.

***

To Sarah Dahman Carlos, my daughter-in-law, for all her patience and support while I borrowed her husband to help me write this book.

***

To Kelly Carlos, my angel, my daughter, whose unconditional love and support has warmed my heart from the very first day she was born, and for creating the LOVE acronym I use in this book.

***

To Michael J. Carlos, my son, my editor, whose insight and wisdom has astonished me. I am thankful for his willingness to show up, edit this book and lovingly share this experience with me. This book is possible and in your hands because of him.

***

I am so blessed, I am so grateful.

Foreword

I first met Noreen when she attended my annual Breakthrough to Success training in Scottsdale, Arizona. She had previously read my book *The Success Principles* and had become interested in my work. When she discovered there was a training to teach the Success Principles her enthusiasm went through the roof. She came back the next year and became a certified Success Principles Trainer. Her deep desire to pay it forward and make a difference in the world resulted in her returning many times to assist and mentor others at my Breakthrough to Success, Train the Trainer, and One Day to Greatness seminars and workshops.

Noreen's enthusiasm and zest for life and her generosity of spirit is contagious and has endeared her to everyone in our community of students and trainers.

Noreen is also one of the people whose stories is featured in my book *Living the Success Principles.* Her story "Mirror Mirror on the Wall, Who Do You Acknowledge Most of All?" demonstrates her dedication to living the Success Principles and the Mirror Exercise, which she has made her own and called it "The Compassionate Mirror Ritual," which she has been practicing daily for over seven years without missing a day. Impressive indeed.

Before I first met Noreen, she had already been inspiring and empowering others for many years through her work as a Weight

Watchers International leader/facilitator, as a yoga teacher and in her own coaching business—Joyfilled Lifestyle.

And now Noreen has taken her commitment to inspire and empower others to create a healthier and more joy-filled life one more step by writing *Living in Joy: Creating Positive Change One Small Glorious Step at a Time.*

Noreen's willingness to be open and vulnerable will take you on an honest journey of feeling pain, moving forward and creating joy. Her generous heart, fun loving spirit and spontaneous sense of humor lends itself well to the stories she shares.

She weaves her personal stories, pain and perspective into a compelling way to honor your well- being, turn your tears into pearls of wisdom, and live in joy.

I encourage you to allow Noreen's stories and discoveries to inspire and empower you to examine your own limiting beliefs and thoughts and create the life you truly desire to be living, in her words, *one small glorious step at a time.*

Jack Canfield
Co-author of the bestselling Chicken Soup for the Soul® series and *The Success Principles™: How to Get from Where You Are to Where You Want to Be*

Dedication

I dedicate this book to my parents, Mae and Frank Kelty, who never knew how their unconditional love and compassionate non-judgment was the best gift they ever could have given me and to my children, Kelly and Michael, who continue to teach me new things about unconditional love and life with each passing day.

Table of Contents

Endorsements 3

Acknowledgements 5

Foreword 9

Dedication 11

Table of Contents 12

Chapter 1: The Truth Will Set You Free 14

Chapter 2: I Am So Grateful 31

Chapter 3: Small Steps Lead to Big Success 45

Chapter 4: You Bring Me Joy... 61

Chapter 5: The Beauty of the Butterfly 72

Chapter 6: Love, Not Fear 80

Chapter 7: You Can't Be in Two Places at the Same Time 92

Chapter 8: Who Holds The Key? 100

Chapter 9: Mirror, Mirror on the Wall, Who Do You Acknowledge Most of All? 107

Chapter 10: I Am So Blessed 114

Chapter 11: I Feel Good! 119

Chapter 12: Our Lives Are The Direct Result Of The Stories We Tell 124

Chapter 13: A Blessing in Disguise..129

Chapter 1: The Truth Will Set You Free

"Facts do not cease to exist because they are ignored." - Aldous Huxley

***

When I was fourteen years old, a subway train struck and killed my father at 50th Street and Broadway in New York City. This tragedy, coupled with a Type I Diabetes diagnosis just a few months earlier, permanently altered the course of my life. Not only would I have to inject myself with an insulin needle every day, but I would also have to soldier through life without the warmth of my father's loving presence. This is the story of how I turned the greatest pain into the most unconditional love.

My father's name was Francis Michael Kelty, but most people called him Frank and those closest to him called him Frankie. He was born in Whitestone, Queens on August 27, 1919, the third of four boys. He grew up to be tall and thin and very handsome. He had hazel eyes and thin black hair that grayed around his temples as he got older. His smile brightened every room he ever walked into. In his younger years, he and his brothers sang at local social gatherings in bars and reception halls all around Queens. They even recorded a version of "Paper Doll", the 1943 song by the Mills Brothers.

After he married my mother, he started working for the NYC Department of Highways, paving roads and filling in potholes as he smoothed the road for others. He always smelled like asphalt when he came home from work and whenever I smell fresh asphalt, it makes me think of him. He also always had cough drops in his pocket. Different flavors, too. Licorice, lemon, cherry, honey. My sisters and I loved when he would share them with us after he came home.

He didn't drive so we went everywhere by bus, subway, taxi, or walking. He loved to walk. We used to take the bus to Coney Island to play skee-ball and eat hot dogs and corn-on-the-cob on the boardwalk. He also liked to take us to Kissena Park in nearby Flushing to ride the ponies.

In the summers, my mother took my sisters and me to stay at my grandparents' beach house two hours away in Laurel, Long Island while my father stayed home and worked. On the weekends, he took the Long Island Railroad out to visit us. My grandmother, whom we called Nana, drove my sisters and me to the station to meet him as soon as his train pulled in. Never one to be late, she always got us there early. As the time ticked by, we became more and more excited to see him. When his train inevitably arrived, he stepped off with a big smile on his face and chocolate candy bars in his hands.

Despite not having much money during our childhood, he loved to give gifts, especially on our birthdays, which he went out of his way to make special for each of us. He let us pick out our own gifts and one year, my younger sister, Patti, and I asked for pogo sticks. He gave us better pogo sticks than we had ever seen before. He always went above and beyond our expectations and took utter delight in surprising us. Patti and I have birthdays that are just a week apart so sometimes my mother would try to get away with one cake for both of us, but my father vehemently objected and always made sure we each got our own cake. I still have a portable typewriter and tape recorder that he gave me for my birthday as well as a birthday party invitation for August 15, 1971 that is in his handwriting.

When I was thirteen, I helped my father paint the kitchen cabinets instead of going to the eighth-grade dance; however, my father didn't want me to miss out on all the fun and insisted I go to the dance with my best friend, Claudia. He had even purchased a black turtleneck that he knew I had my eye on and gave it to me to wear to the dance. He had such a loving nature and always made me feel appreciated.

My father loved baseball and the New York Mets in particular. He shared that love with my sisters and me. The first year that I really paid attention was 1969, the year that the Miracle Mets won their first World Series. My father and I watched most of the games on TV and hearing those TV announcers after he died made me feel closer to him. My father also liked to take us to Opening Day at Shea Stadium, where he had a part-time job as a security guard. One year, he got sick and couldn't go so my mother had to take us instead. It was a brutally cold day and we kept getting up from our seats to go get hot chocolate. We finally gave in and went home before the end of the game. My mother didn't even really like baseball back then, but she started watching all the games after my father died, perhaps as a way of keeping her connection with him. In some respects, the Mets played that role for all of us.

During the 1980s, my older sister, Kathy, took her fandom to a new level, following the Mets as they got better and better, culminating in their first World Series victory since 1969 when they beat the Boston Red Sox in 1986. She also landed her dream job when she became a nurse in the Shea Stadium First Aid Office in April 1993. Her favorite player was first baseman Keith Hernandez. I will never forget about the time that she found her way onto the field during his Mets Hall of Fame induction ceremony. I was at work when I got a call from my kids, Kelly and Michael, who were 8 at the time. They had been watching the induction ceremony on TV when they saw their Aunt Kathy standing on the field with Keith Hernandez and other Mets legends.

At around the same time, my husband, Mike, and I restarted the family tradition of going to Opening Day each year. We checked the kids out of school early to sit behind home plate in seats Kathy got for us through her job at the stadium. One year, she took Kelly and Michael down into the hallway that led to the clubhouses and dugouts and introduced them to a few of the players. Kathy gave them an experience they'll never forget and made Kelly and Michael Mets fans for life, ensuring that my father's love of the Mets was passed on to the next generation as well.

Another thing my father shared with us was his love of Christmas. Some of my fondest memories of him take me back to his fun, playful demeanor around the holidays. He liked to sip blackberry brandy and sing "White Christmas," his voice sounding just like Bing Crosby, full of Christmas cheer. He also liked to go to the neighbors' houses and help them put together toys for their children. Every year, we walked up to the vacant lot on the corner of 17th Road and 150th Street to pick out our Christmas tree. Once we found the perfect one, my sisters and I helped my father carry it back home, singing Christmas songs as we walked. The house always felt so vibrant as he placed the tree in the stand and we helped him decorate it with lights, ornaments, and tinsel.

For so many years, I remembered my father by his death. By writing this book with my son and sharing these details about my father, I'm able to remember him by his life, one that was lived joyfully.

***

On New Year's Eve 1972, my sisters and I gathered around the Christmas tree in the living room with my parents. Mom made a canned ham, her famous potato salad, and homemade apple pie. We had lots of snacks, including Ritz crackers and Kraft pimento cheese spread, a special treat reserved only for New Year's Eve in our house. We watched Dick Clark's New Year's Eve Special on TV and counted down until the ball dropped in Times Square. We shouted, "Happy New Year!" and kissed each other. This was the last time all six of us were in the same room together.

On Saturday, January 6, 1973, I helped my father take down our Christmas tree before walking to the bus stop to wait for a bus to take me to my grandparents' house in Fresh Meadows, where Kathy and I were staying at the time. As I waited, I watched my parents and my eight-year-old sister, Maryann, walk in the other direction on their way to St. Luke's Church for five o'clock Mass. With each step that they took, my father faded farther from my view until he was no longer visible. Little did I know that would be the last time I saw him.

What happened next is extremely unclear. Nobody knows when he left, but he wasn't home when my mother woke up on Sunday morning. My sister, Patti, says that later that night he said goodbye to her before sneaking out the back window to go have a few drinks, which he was known to do on occasion. He would say he was going to mail a letter or get a pizza and then call my mother from the bar down the street (which conveniently served pizza) to say that he'd be home soon. He'd come home a few hours later with a pizza for everyone but we all knew he had been drinking.

What made this time different is that he never called. When he still hadn't come home by Sunday night, my mother called my grandparents to figure out what to do. After school on Monday, my grandparents told me, "The family needs to be together," and took Kathy and me back to my parents' house on 17th Road.

Over the next few days, my mother and my grandparents frantically called friends, relatives, and local hospitals to try to track him down and filed a missing person report with the local police department. As each day passed, the whole family grew more and more concerned and we began to sense that something terrible must have happened.

We were all home from school in observance of Martin Luther King, Jr. Day on Monday, January 15th. It had been over a week since anybody had seen my father. At that point, although I clung to a sliver of hope that he was still out there somewhere, we were all pretty much just waiting to hear the bad news. Every time the phone rang, we froze in anticipation for what the call would bring. Was it him? Was it the police? Had somebody found him?

My sister Maryann and I were on the porch fooling around and singing a very silly song called "Chantilly Lace" when my mother received a call from the New York City Morgue and my whole world came to a screeching halt.

My mother told me that they had an unidentified body found on January 7. My heart stopped as time stood still for a moment. She told me that my grandparents were on their way to pick her up and drive her into the city with my sister Kathy, who was ten days shy of her eighteenth birthday. She told me to stay home with Maryann. My other sister, Patti, who was 13 at the time, was out with friends. After waiting for what seemed like hours (although it couldn't have been more than an hour and a half), I went into the bathroom and sobbed into the towel on the rack, thinking that if it wasn't him they would have called me by now.

When my mother finally walked back into the house, she hugged me as she delivered the bad news and I began to sob again, but then I saw my grandparents gesturing with their hands to stop crying. Of course, my sisters and I still went through a whole box of tissues as we cried later that night.

The next day would have been my parents' 19th wedding anniversary, but instead we held a wake for my father. My father always gave my mother a rose for each year that they were married. This year, she laid 19 roses on his casket. For the first hour of the wake, everyone kept very quiet. Nobody knew how to behave under such circumstances so we all kept up the pretense of being strong for each other. The tension in the room was palpable until my father's Uncle Dan burst into the room with tears in his eyes, threw himself on the casket and screamed "FRAANKIEEEEE!!!!". He expressed the devastation and heartache we were all feeling but refused to acknowledge. In that moment, I felt understood. He had validated my pain. What a wonderful release. His actions inspired me to always to be fully present at wakes and funerals and to allow space for grieving. Be present. Be a shoulder to cry on and give your shoulder to someone else. Share the support and share the pain. No pretense.

Prior to my father's wake, I had only confronted death once before, after his mother passed away six years earlier. Grandma Kelty was Uncle Dan's sister and they lived together when I was a little girl. Uncle Dan used to walk me home from school every day during the first grade and I would make homemade eggnog by mixing up milk, egg, vanilla and sugar. Then I'd pour it into a glass milk bottle to bring to Grandma Kelty's house, which was just three houses down from ours on 17th Road in Whitestone. I grew very close to her during these afternoon visits. She was always 100% present with me and made me feel loved. After she died, my parents let me choose whether to go to her wake. Even though I was only 8 at the time, I knew that I wanted to attend.

I don't remember the trip from my house to Gleason's Funeral Home, but what I remember vividly is carefully approaching the kneeler and kneeling next to her casket. She looked serene, dressed in a beautiful lilac dress with rosary beads wrapped around her smooth hands. I noticed her hands because when she was alive she suffered from arthritis and her knuckles looked swollen all the time. Now, she seemed to be at peace. I was so grateful my parents allowed me to go. To this day, I still have a set of her rosary beads that she kept in a leather case inscribed with the words, "My Companion".

***

We all had our own way of avoiding the pain of my father's death. The wounds were too big and too deep, so we barely even talked about my father in the following years. My mother turned to valium. Kathy, Patti, and I drank more and started to smoke pot. Maryann was too young for drugs or alcohol; instead, she spent countless hours at her friend's house. My older sister, Kathy, opened up to our high school guidance counselor, Mr. Canzoniero, and encouraged me to do the same, but I was still too deep in denial to start the healing process. My father had a closed casket at his funeral, so it was easy for me to fantasize that he was still alive. I took on the role of the "good little soldier," accepting all the responsibilities of the house and getting a part-time job to help make ends meet. But none of it filled the void left by the loss of my father and his steady presence.

After high school, Kathy graduated Flushing Hospital's School of Nursing and obtained a job in the hospital's Labor & Delivery department, where she worked for the next 35+ years. Patti and I also moved out after high school and rented an apartment together on Long Island. We both had jobs at the Pathmark supermarket in Whitestone, where I met my husband, Mike. He was the Customer Service Manager at the time and hired Patti as a cashier the summer after she graduated high school. I had already been working there since 1973 and he had been there since 1975, but we didn't begin dating until Christmas 1977. He proposed while we were out to dinner for my 22nd birthday at Windows on the World, the restaurant at the top of the World Trade Center building. We got married at St. Mary's Church in Flushing on July 25, 1981. Just a few months later, I rescued a mixed-breed puppy named Scooter, whom I thought of as my first child. I've had other dogs in my life, but none as loving or as special to me. She provided comfort when I needed it most and was always by my side. A year later, Maryann graduated high school and followed in Kathy's footsteps by getting a job working as a Dietary Aide at Flushing Hospital.

Mike and I rang in Christmas 1985 by buying a house in East Meadow, a small hamlet located within the Town of Hempstead on Long Island, about 30 miles east of Manhattan. At the time, my life was unfolding just as I had always imagined. I had gotten married, I had a good job, and we had just purchased our first home. After a few years of just the two of us plus Scooter in the house, we decided to have children.

Sixteen years after my father's death, almost to the day, I found out that I was pregnant. The date was Friday the 13th of January 1989 and ever since, the number 13 has been a very lucky number for me. It was also a lucky number for my husband, Mike, whose own father had been born in 1913. I knew that getting pregnant would be challenging because of the diabetes, but it was worth it because I wanted to have children. My doctor told me that the tighter control I had over my diabetes at the time of conception, the better the chances would be for the baby, so he put me on four daily short acting insulin injections to give me better control.

In April 1989, I found out that I was having twins and the pregnancy became double high risk. Not only did I have to manage my diabetes, but I also had to be concerned with two babies now. It would have been easy to become twice as scared, but instead I had double the joy, double the determination. Although I was due on September 7, the doctor wanted me to stop working on May 1. He also wanted me to start monitoring my contractions then. Once a day, I placed a belt around my belly to record contractions for 60 minutes and then sent the info from the device to a monitoring company via telephone. The technology was probably modern at the time but now it sounds archaic. On May 25, after sending that day's results, I received a call from the monitoring company. The woman on the phone told me to drink a glass of water and repeat the 60-minute recording. After repeating the whole process and sending those results, I received another call and this time, she told me that the doctor wanted me to meet him at Flushing Hospital in Queens, which was about a 30-minute drive away from our house on Long Island. Mike drove and when we arrived, I was admitted to the hospital and told I was in labor. "I am only 25 weeks. How could I be in labor?" I thought. The doctors initially stopped the contractions with magnesium sulfate. After a few days, they sent me home with a Terbutaline pump to prevent further contractions and instructed me to stay on total bedrest.

At this time, Mike and I decided it would be best if we stayed at Nana's house in Fresh Meadows, which was less than ten minutes away from the hospital. We thought it was a great idea because Nana was staying out east at her summer house. We packed up our things and moved in along with our dog, Scooter.

While I was banned from activity and on total bedrest, only allowed to get up to go to the bathroom, my sisters and my mother really came to the rescue. They made a calendar and made sure someone was always with me while my husband was at work. I never felt so loved and supported. When I reflect on this, I realize it was remarkable the way that we all came together so cohesively. The timing couldn't have been better. Kathy and Maryann were both working at Flushing Hospital and my other sister, Patti, was living downstairs at Nana's house.

As I felt this new life fluttering in my belly, like a butterfly flapping her wings, an overwhelming feeling of love began to permeate and soften the wall that I had put up 16 years before. Although most times we view being overwhelmed as a negative feeling, this time it brought me joy. As a family, we began taking small steps towards ensuring the birth of two healthy babies.

We spent the next six weeks paving the way for their arrival. On July 27, 1989 I gave birth via emergency C-section to twins, a girl and a boy. Kelly Michele was born first, weighing 3 lbs., 13.5 ounces, followed by Michael John, weighing 4 lbs., 15.5 ounces. Because they were born six weeks early, they were taken to the intensive care nursery and placed on heart monitors. Michael had more complications than Kelly. As I laid in bed recovering the next day, my husband came into the room with tears in his eyes. I jumped out of the bed so fast I nearly ripped my stitches out. I asked him, "What happened?" He replied, "They're working on Michael. They asked me to leave." Apparently, Michael had water around his lungs. The doctors had to insert two tubes into his tiny chest to drain the fluid. I prayed to God and asked, "Please don't leave him here for a few days and then take him away." The next day, when I woke up and Michael was still fighting to stay alive, I suddenly had faith that everything would be okay. My prayers had been answered. I wasn't allowed to hold him in my arms but felt it was very important to keep my hands in the incubator touching his frail little body. Wires were everywhere, and he had a tube in his mouth and two tubes in his chest, but I made sure I kept my hands in there, thinking "He's gotta be held, he's gotta be held." A baby needs his mother's touch.

On August 15th, one of the nurses said, "Sit there, I'm gonna do something for you." Then she gently unhooked Michael from all the wires and removed him from the incubator. She placed him in my arms and began re-attaching all the wires, allowing me to hold him for the very first time. Knowing this was a very special gift, she beamed at me with an excited smile and said, "Happy Birthday!!" It was one of the best birthday presents I have ever received. I finally got to hold my baby boy.

A week later, we brought Kelly home from the hospital and one of my neighbors said that she was so small she could fit in a shoebox. We were concerned about how Scooter would react to the new baby, so I knelt down as I entered the house and calmly invited Scooter to come meet Kelly. She carefully approached and sniffed a bit. I pet her and introduced her to our new addition to the family. I couldn't believe how gentle she was with her. Her reaction was so natural. It was like Kelly had always been part of the family.

Three days after that, we brought Michael home too. Again, I knelt down and introduced Michael to Scooter. She responded to Michael the same way that she had to Kelly. Once again, it was like he had always been part of the family. For the next few months, Kelly and Michael each slept in a bassinet on either side of our bed. Whenever they were asleep, Scooter would jump up on the bed, walk over to one side and check the bassinet. Then she would walk over to the other side and check the other bassinet. Once she had checked on both of them, she would lie down in the middle of the bed like she was guarding them.

Kelly and Michael brought so much love and joy that my heart began to melt and so did the walls I had so carefully built and maintained to guard against the pain from my father's death. For years, I had stuffed all the feelings down to avoid that pain.

After becoming a parent, I started to examine my father's choices through a new lens. As I crossed the train tracks driving home from work one night, I thought of my father and felt profound sadness, questioning, "How could someone become so hopeless?" I reflected on the holiday season prior to his death and thought about how sad he seemed. His behavior at the time scared me because it was not like him at all. He was normally happy, animated and full of life. He loved to have fun and was always singing around the house. But during those few months just before his death, he became quiet, sullen, almost withdrawn--and very concerned with money.

This is when I finally began the real grieving process. Kelly and Michael were 3 at the time and I said to myself, "You can't *feel* all this love without feeling the pain." I decided to share fun stories about my father with my kids. I began framing black and white photos from both my family and my husband's family. My father loved taking photos and I still have the camera he purchased with his first paycheck from a job he had at EDO Aircraft during his twenties. The reason I had so many old photos was because he was always taking pictures. When I hung all the framed photos in the hallway of our house, they took up a whole wall. I started the project because it was fun, but I soon realized just how cathartic it was for me to connect with my father in this way and share his joy with my children.

A couple years later, I helped my mother sell the family home on 17th road where we grew up. I filmed Kelly and Michael, now 5, as we walked through all the rooms and the backyard telling stories from my childhood. I invited my sisters for one last Easter before we closed on the house in June. I found baskets like the ones we had when we were little and made Easter baskets for everyone.

Selling a house is a very significant life event. It is much more than an exchange of money for goods. We have to let go of things that contain so much emotion, so many memories. But the truth is that we hold the people and the memories in our hearts forever. I told my sisters the date of the closing and the time of the final walkthrough with the buyers. All of them said they could not make it, but on the day of the closing, one by one, they each showed up. The house on 17th Road was the last place we shared time with our father. It felt like we were saying goodbye all over again.

Although I began to grieve my father's death around this time, I didn't have an honest talk with Kelly and Michael about my father and the possibilities about what really happened until they were in college. One day, while they were home on a semester break, I sat them down and we had a deep conversation during which I shared some details they didn't know about and told them that my father might have taken his own life. I felt relieved to have shared this with them. My kids are such an important part of my life. I felt that now that they were adults, they should know the truth about their grandfather.

A few months later in November 2009, I attended Yoga Teacher Training at the Kripalu Center for Yoga & Health in the Berkshires. During this training, we were doing meditation, partner exercises and opening the heart exercises. After my first practice teach, Jurian, one of the teachers who observed me, told me I was a reverse breather. She assigned Sarah, one of the assistants, to work with me during the lunch break. Sarah started by saying, "Sometimes something scares us, we hold our breath and then we become reverse breathers." She continued speaking, but I was still processing the words "something scares us". I was thinking, "Yes, I never processed the 'scared' of my father's death or the time before it." I asked her to stop and shared what I was thinking. I said, "My father took his own life". After saying it, I realized that those words had never crossed my lips before. Even when I spoke to Kelly and Michael, I said, "might have". I shared the story the next day with two more people and felt liberated. I thought my healing was done.

Then, a few years later, my son Michael emailed me a story he published on a flash fiction blog called Underwater Minefield that he worked on with some friends from college. As I began reading, my palms started to sweat, my heart beat a little faster, and I felt my body tense up. Although the names had been changed and some of the info had been tweaked a little, it was the story of my father leaving the house and approaching the subway. Michael is an exceptional writer, so his words put me right in the experience, and he kept writing, "Breathe in, breathe out." After reading the story, I became very unsettled and thought he should not have shared this private story. I called him, angry and upset, and asked him to take it down, which he did. Years later, with his permission, here is Michael's story:

"Breathe in, breathe out.

These were the words Frank had been reminding himself of for the past few days. It began Friday morning when he punched his timecard at the Queens construction depot where he had worked for the past eight years. Breathe in, breathe out.

He slid his orange hat on to his head and climbed into the seat of the steamroller to begin smoothing over the fresh asphalt on Northern Boulevard. Breathe in, breathe out.

The construction site's thick, putrid air hung in his tired old lungs. When the day was done, he left his helmet in his locker, ran a grimy hand through thinning, oily hair and looked in the mirror, catching a brief glimpse of the man he had become. Breathe in, breathe out.

That night, Frank had dinner in his Whitestone home with his wife, Mildred, and their four daughters. After the meal, he walked Louise and Mary to the bus stop around the corner. They had been living with their grandmother in Corona for the past few months because they couldn't stand to live with their mother. This broke Frank's heart. He watched sorrowfully as his teenage daughters, just on the verge of high school, climbed on to the bus and disappeared inside. Mary peered out the back window and watched her dejected father slump back towards the house. Breathe in, breathe out.

Later that night, once everyone had gone to sleep, Frank visited each of their rooms. He watched eight-year old Helen toss and turn in her sleep. He saw

Florence, his oldest at eighteen, snore peacefully in the bed he had built for her when she was just a little girl. Breathe in, breathe out.

He leaned in the doorway of his bedroom and looked at his wife of twenty years. He remembered the day he had first laid eyes on her at a church dance. He eventually summoned the courage to ask her to dance. She said yes. The next night they went out to the boardwalk at Jones Beach and talked until the sun came up. That morning, he drove over to his brother's house in College Point and told him about how he had met the woman he knew he would someday marry. Now he just leaned in and kissed her gently on her forehead—she was a sleeping beauty still, even at forty-seven. Breathe in, breathe out.

As he pulled the front door closed, his heart thumped and his throat lumped. Breathe in, breathe out.

He caught a cab into Manhattan and roamed the streets of Midtown that he had known so well in his youth. He stopped off at a club in Hell's Kitchen where he had sung the songs of Bing Crosby and Nat King Cole with his brothers and had even cut a record of "Paper Doll." He ordered an old-fashioned, sipped it thoughtfully for a moment and then drank it down. He left a crumpled bill on the bar and walked outside. Breathe in, breathe out.

He lit a cigarette as he entered the subway station at 50th and Broadway. Breathe in, breathe out.

He descended the steps, slipped a token in the slot, and moved through the turnstile. Breathe in, breathe out.

He glanced at his wristwatch. 3:52 AM. Breathe in, breathe out.

He stamped out his cigarette and moved to the edge of the platform. Breathe in, breathe out.

He peered down the dark tunnel to see if a train was coming. Breathe in, breathe out.

Two white lights crept into view. Breathe in, breathe out.

He took a step. Breathe in—"

Very powerful story.

It's been a long journey from the extreme pain of my father's death to the acceptance and understanding to move forward and appreciate the value of sharing.

One of the major breakthroughs in this journey happened while attending Jack Canfield's 7-day "Breakthrough to Success" event in Arizona in August 2011. I had read his book, "The Success Principles", in 2009 and absolutely loved it. I started using the Principles in my personal and professional life and signed up for his email newsletter. I first read about the Breakthrough to Success event in one of those newsletters and knew that I really wanted to go. I couldn't make it in 2009 or 2010, but I did get the chance to meet Jack at an event in Boston in 2010, which strengthened my resolve to attend the next year. In 2011, I was finally able to attend. On the second day of the event, Jack surprised me by calling me up on stage while the entire group of 200+ attendees sang "Happy Birthday". I was turning 53, the same age my father was when he died. As I looked out at the sea of smiling, singing faces full of joy, I thought, "I am rewriting history". Since then, I've attended and even assisted at other events Jack has held and consider him to be a mentor and friend.

One of Jack's Success Principles is Tell the Truth Faster; however, it has taken me over 5 years and dozens of trainings and workshops to come to the conclusion that my initial reaction to my son's short story was only an indication there was more healing to do around my father's death and the beliefs I learned as a child. I now speak very freely about my father's death. Once shared, the shame no longer holds any power. In fact, there is no shame. To the contrary, I've found that sharing my story creates connection with others and provides a basis for support, but I never discussed it with my son until after being diagnosed with Multiple Sclerosis in December 2016. The diagnosis created a newfound sense of urgency around the desire to write my book and I knew that I wanted my son's help to do it.

In January 2017, almost 44 years to the day of my father's death, I called my son and apologized for my initial reaction to the short story he wrote in 2011. In hindsight, I thought that I might have dimmed his light about writing, which was the last thing I wanted to do. I've always strived to inspire Michael to follow his dreams and pursue his passions. Michael is an exceptional writer and it bothered me that I may have done something to discourage his gift due to my own limitations. I then asked him to write this book with me and allow me to include his story, "Breathe Out." Michael agreed and said, "I've been waiting for you to ask me to help you write your book." He seemed even more excited than I was.

We got to the truth faster and it set us free to embark on the creation of this book together. **Our first meeting about the book was Jan. 16, 2017. January 16 the day my parents were wed in 1954 and 43 years after that first day of my father's wake.

Chapter 2: I Am So Grateful

"A grateful mind is a great mind, which eventually attracts to itself great things." - Plato

***

My mother, Mae Noreen Scully, was born in Corona, New York on March 31, 1926. She married my father on January 16, 1954 and gave birth to Kathleen Frances, the first of four daughters, on January 25, 1955. I was second in line, born in Parsons Hospital in Flushing on August 15, 1958, a day celebrated as the Feast of the Assumption of Mary in the Catholic religion. I've always felt a special connection to Parsons Hospital and to Mary, which is both my middle name and the name of my father's mother, who also just happened to die in Parsons Hospital. When I got married, we held the wedding at St. Mary's Church on Parsons Boulevard, just a few blocks from where Parsons Hospital used to stand. When I had kids, they were born at Flushing Hospital, just a few blocks further up on Parsons Boulevard.

After I was born, next came Patricia Ann, less than a year later on August 8, 1959. Patti and I were 51 weeks apart, which was how my mother would introduce us to new people. Patti and I would just roll our eyes, but we have always had a special relationship because of how close we are in age. Maryann was the last of four daughters, born on September 16, 1964. The four of us provided my mother with endless challenges throughout her life but also gave her so many moments of joy and love.

In the summer of 1964, my mother took my sisters and me out to Long Island for a day at Jones Beach. She was pregnant with Maryann at the time and wore a flowy white dress with big red flowers on it. This was one of the first times I ever visited Jones Beach, where my parents went on their first date, and one of my earliest memories of my mother. She held my sister, Patti, and me by the hand and led us out to the water's edge. We planted our feet deeply into the sand and watched as the waves rolled in over our feet. As the waves rolled back out, I could feel the water and the sand being pulled from between my toes. It almost felt like our feet would be pulled out with the waves as well, but my mother stood firm and tightly gripped our hands. I stared up at her with awe, thinking about how pretty she looked. She had a big smile on her face as she watched us giggle each time the waves rolled back in over our feet. She made me feel so safe.

As a child, I didn't feel this way very often. I wanted her to be more nurturing or offer more guidance and discipline. It wasn't until after I became a mother myself that I began to appreciate the way she allowed me to be independent and follow my own path. She empowered me to do the same with my own children. She always welcomed our friends into our home and made them feel comfortable. She loved when we had parties, saying, "At least, I know you are safe and at home." After my father died, she had to raise four daughters all by herself. That's nothing to sneeze at.

After Kelly and Michael were born, my mother was the happiest I had ever witnessed her to be. She was always smiling and thoroughly appreciated her time with them. She was always telling me, "They tug on my heart."

In hindsight, I have nothing but admiration for her for all the things she had to handle on her own. I am grateful to her for allowing me to grow into the person I would eventually become.

A great example of how she helped shaped my outlook on life came when I was in the first grade. My mother was concerned because I was a little quiet (oh, how the times have changed!) and seemed shy, so she put me in the St. Patrick's Day play at St. Luke's Church. My group danced and sang, "I want to go back to my little grass shack in Kealakekua, Hawaii."

I had so much fun that I participated in the play again the following year and sang, "Happy Talk," from the musical *South Pacific*:

> *Happy talk, keep talking happy talk,*
>
> *Talk about things you'd like to do,*
>
> *You gotta have a dream, if you don't have a dream,*
>
> *How are you gonna have a dream come true?*

The seed was planted. I have been singing and believing that ever since.

***

To understand my mother, you need to know more about her parents. Her mother, Mildred, whom the grandkids all called "Nana," was the matriarch of the family. Nana was about 5'9" with brown eyes and light brown hair. She was always impeccably dressed, wearing matching pearl earrings and beads around her neck. She was a fabulous cook and kept her home in perfect order. When she was eighty-six years old, she was still very active, wallpapering the bathroom in her house all by herself. My sisters, cousins, and I all looked up to Nana for her strength. She was a mover and a shaker who took great pride in maintaining her two homes, the house in Queens and the summer house on the eastern tip of Long Island in Laurel, New York. Beautiful flowers adorned both homes. She even brought me a beautiful bouquet of flowers freshly picked from her garden when she came to my house to meet Kelly and Michael for the first time. Back in the 60's and 70's, she ran the family's summer house so efficiently. There were ten grandchildren to go along with her two kids and their spouses. There was so much for her to coordinate, yet everything ran as smooth as silk.

As the grandchildren grew older, we started to split the summer so my family had July and my cousins had August, but both families came together for our big 4th of July celebration. The house was on the water of Peconic Bay. We always had spare ribs on the barbecue for dinner. Later in the night, we would all sit on the lawn watching the boats traveling to the boatyard west of us to watch the fireworks. That lawn provided front row seats for the most beautiful fireworks show of the year. The cousins would light sparklers and drop them in a pail of water that Nana had strategically placed on the lawn to keep us safe. We roasted marshmallows and ate caramel corn and watermelon as we watched the fireworks. Then we would watch all the boats with their lights beaming pass our house on their trip back home. All part of the experience Nana had curated for us.

Nana liked to go to Bingo on Monday nights. When Patti and I were about eleven or twelve, she started taking us with her. As a special treat, she would place hard candies in the middle of the table--sometimes butterscotch, sometimes root beer. If any of us won or even got close to winning, we felt so excited. When we came home at almost 11:00 pm, she would still serve my grandfather a cup of tea, something for dessert and fill him in on all the neighborhood gossip.

My grandfather, John, or as the grandchildren called him, "Popa," was about 5'7" and medium in build. He walked with a bit of a limp because one leg was shorter than the other. He even wore special shoes with a larger heel on one shoe. By the time I knew him, he had gray hair, gorgeous baby blue eyes, and a wonderful smile. He smoked Muriel air tip cigars so whenever I see a discarded air tip cigar at a park or beach, I think it is him giving me a little wink. Popa was a man ahead of his time. He had an answering machine for his phone before anyone else, which sounds so archaic but in 1971 was unheard of. He held all kinds of jobs through the years but in his retirement years had his own business, Scully Investigations, which eventually evolved into a staffing agency for security guards. When he went to Florida for the winter, my mother would oversee the business, handling phone calls and delegating the weekly payroll to thirteen-year-old me. I was so excited to help and thoroughly enjoyed writing the weekly payroll checks for the guards. Two of the accounts I remember were for Queens College and Mack Truck. Helping with the business made me feel so strong, smart and capable.

Popa was so proud of his cars, always using a special buffing cloth to get them nice and shiny in the driveway at the beach house. He drove a Mercedes-Benz that he traded in every two years for a new one, insisting on having the vanity license plate JTS-6. JTS were his initials John Thomas Scully. Nana once told us that as a young girl she used to sit on the corner in Queens and watch the cars go by, thinking, "One day, I'm going to own one of those." After they got married, Popa made her dream come true. He liked to say, "Nana acts like I'm in charge but we all know she's the boss." They were married for nearly 60 years and celebrated both their 25th and 50th wedding anniversaries at the waterfront property he'd purchased in 1950. They both loved that house so much and put so much blood, sweat, and tears into making it a special place for their kids and grandkids. There was a pebble road from the house up to the main street until Popa decided to pay to have it paved sometime in the 1960s. Because he paid for it, the town let him name the road. He dug the hole and inserted the signpost that read, "Maple Lane," into the ground himself. That signpost has since been replaced but the name lives on.

My grandfather loved to sit around the table at dinnertime and tell stories about his sisters, his mother and our family history. He also loved to teach us. He would tell us the Spanish names for things on the dinner table. My best friend, Claudia, said the thing she loved about my grandfather was he always made us think. I agree. He was a great storyteller--animated, funny but always had teaching points. He was always asking us questions.

He referred many times to a book he had on a shelf in his home in Fresh Meadows called "How to Win Friends and Influence People" by

Dale Carnegie. I loved the title and all the information he shared from the book. At an early age, I became a big fan of Dale Carnegie. Many years later when I was a member of Toastmasters, I gave a speech on the importance of remembering people's names. I opened with a line from that book that always stuck with me: "Remember that a person's name is to that person the sweetest and most important sound in any language".

Popa was an extraordinary man, a visionary, a man ahead of his time.

***

My grandparents always came over to our house for Thanksgiving, which was one of my favorite holidays growing up. When I was about eleven or twelve years old, I woke up early Thanksgiving morning to the intoxicating aroma of the turkey already basting in the oven. I jumped up, quickly showered and got dressed so I could head downstairs. Mom was already in the kitchen, sitting at the table peeling and chopping turnips and potatoes. Five pots were on top of the stove, each designated for a vegetable or a cream sauce waiting to be made. The turkey was already stuffed and in the oven. Burgundy and white bags from Stork's Bakery sat on top of the fridge. Inside the bags rested fresh rye bread and crumb cake. Mom wore an apron, sweat on her brow from the heat of the kitchen. My sisters and father gathered in the living room to watch the Thanksgiving Day Parade on TV.

We were expecting Nana and Popa at noon. Mom placed her Irish linen tablecloth on the dining room table after she and my dad put the leaves in the table. She gave my sisters and me the china and the wooden case with the good silverware to set the table. Then we got the glasses and linen napkins out of the china closet. Mom placed special oblong glass dishes on the table with celery, green olives and sweet gherkin pickles just before Nana and Popa arrived. It was all part of the ritual.

Once the turkey came out of the oven, it was time to start the gravy. She had been timing the vegetables perfectly, placing sweet potatoes in the oven and making cream sauce for the vegetables. She coordinated everything so effortlessly, allowing the day's events to unfold so smoothly. Dad carved the turkey, and everything seemed to be going on the table just as he entered the dining room with the platter of turkey.

After all these years, I still remember the smells so vividly. The meal was absolutely scrumptious, a very special meal indeed.

After dinner, Nana, my sisters and I did the dishes. Homemade pies and ice cream were served for dessert. My favorite was apple pie with a scoop of vanilla ice cream from a local ice cream parlor called Bertleson's in Whitestone Village, just a few doors down from Stork's Bakery. All part of the tradition. Nana would stop for the ice cream because Popa liked the maple walnut ice cream from Bertleson's.

After dessert, we played canasta, the card game Nana taught us during lazy summer nights out at the beach house. Canasta has many rules, maybe even too many, but Nana had mastered them all and was a great canasta player. I liked to sit next to her and watch how she played her hand, which cards she held on to. She always seemed to pick up big packs and go on to win the game. Canasta is played with partners. Sometimes the pack would build up, everyone discarding but nobody picking it up. You would need to hold two of the same cards to pick up the deck. If you pick it up, then you get to use all the cards in the deck. If it was a large pack, then there would be many cards to make canastas and build points. The tension would build if it went around to all four people a few times in a row with nobody picking it up. As we played on Thanksgiving, this exact scenario played out. Mom and I were partners and the pack was very large. Suddenly, Mom held her discard up and said, "I am going to take a stab in the dark," which did not sound too promising to me. Of course, my sister Patti was just waiting for her to put the card down hoping she could get the pack, but Patti did not pick up the pack. The hand went around to my mother and again she holds up her discard and says, "I am going to take a stab in the dark." We all laughed as Patti picked up the pack this time, eventually winning the game. There are so many idiosyncratic phrases my mother used to say that would make Patti and me laugh. Now that we're older and my mom has passed on, I sometimes catch myself saying, "We'll cross that bridge when we come to it," or "Come hell or high water," and I can't help but think of her and laugh.

After canasta, it was time for turkey sandwiches on the Stork's rye bread. Another Thanksgiving in the books, more memories made thanks to my mother's hard work. I may not have fully appreciated it back then, but I'm grateful for that extra mile she put in to make our family's Thanksgiving traditions special.

***

Throughout my teens and twenties, my relationship with my mother was sometimes turbulent. After my father's death, I felt obligated to take care of her, but felt like my efforts were not appreciated. Expressions of gratitude from either of us were few and far between. One such rare moment occurred a few years after my father died when my sister Patti and I re-did the interior of our house. We put up new contact paper on all the walls in the kitchen and bathrooms, painted all of our kitchen cabinets, and cleaned the entire house from floor-to-ceiling. My mother lit up when she walked into our living room and saw a brand-new matching furniture set: couch, loveseat, armchair, coffee table, and two end tables. We were so proud of ourselves and thought that Dad would have appreciated our hard work since he had always been the one who took care of the house. Everything just felt renewed and refreshed.

The feeling was fleeting. My mother had light brown eyes like her mother and those eyes could tell you so much. During the period between my father's death and the time I became pregnant, her eyes were filled with constant uncertainty and struggle. During my pregnancy however, I saw another side of my mother. She was patient and kind, doting on my every need while I was on bedrest and couldn't do things for myself. I think she was happy to be needed and to have someone to take care of. And she was so excited to be becoming a grandmother.

***

My mother had a tough life. Her parents loved and supported her, but they always favored her brother, Jack, who became a doctor and cast a long shadow. She idolized Jack but always felt like, in comparison to him, she could never do anything right in their eyes.

She always had low confidence and lacked self-esteem, which for years I thought was because of her relationship with her parents and brother. Still, I questioned how she could be so unsure of herself because in so many ways she was such a strong woman. Then one day, it all became much clearer. I was at work at Pathmark Supermarkets. It was 1997 we still had wall phones at the store. I was paged to the front of the store for a call. I picked up the call and was surprised to find my mother on the other end of the line. Amid the din of the cash registers and the beeping of the scanners, I listened to her say I have something to tell you, "When I was eight years old and we were on vacation in Massachusetts, a 15-year-old boy from the neighborhood took me for a walk. He told me to take down my pants and he stuck his penis in. It wasn't violent or anything. When I got home, I told my parents. My mother said I had to go to confession. My father wanted to go find the kid and beat the heck out of him and my grandmother held, kissed and cuddled me. Well, okay, my therapist said I should tell my daughters the story, so now I have told all my daughters. Ok, you can go back to work now."

Then she hung up. I just stood there with the phone in my hand, completely flabbergasted, stunned not only by the news but also in her way of delivering it. I hung up the phone, took a deep breath and attempted to gather my thoughts.

At the same time as I began to understand so much more about my mother and her history, I was completely shook. What a way to receive this news. My daughter was the same age at the time as my mother was when her world was completely shattered. I could not even fathom this happening to Kelly and felt such deep empathy for my mother. Still in disbelief, I had to gather myself together and get back to work.

When I got home that night, I wrote my mother a six-page letter on stationery that had pretty purple flowers on it. I wrote to her of my deep love, compassion and admiration for all she had been through in life. I told her she was stronger than she ever gave herself credit for. I thought maybe this might all be coming up for her because my children were now eight years old. I felt totally shattered and sad for her.

I was happy she had her grandmother to comfort her because it didn't sound like her mother comforted her. I made up my own story about Nana's anger, fear and old-fashioned beliefs that made her respond the way she did because I did not understand it at all. Nana was ninety-two and in assisted living at the time, so I could hardly be angry at her, but I certainly felt anger about the situation.

My grandfather never took the family to Massachusetts for vacation again. And that led to the family renting on Long Island out past Riverhead, where he eventually purchased the waterfront property on Peconic Bay. The beach house became a wonderful gathering place for both my family and our cousins for many years to come.

My gratitude, admiration, and compassion for my mom had increased once I had my own children but after that earth-shattering conversation with her, I felt something beyond anything I had experienced before. Deep gratitude. I was so thankful that she shared her pain with me and hoped that, in doing so, perhaps that pain had been eased for her.

***

On Friday, May 7, 2010, which also happened to be Nana's birthday, I received a call from my sister Patti to tell me that my mother was taken to the hospital with shortness of breath and that she was possibly suffering from pneumonia. My mother was eighty-four at this point so things like this happened every once in a while. She was living in an amazing assisted living facility in Queens Village called Queen of Peace. They would take her to Mercy Hospital, where she would be on oxygen for a few days and given antibiotics.

I went to visit her in the hospital on Sunday for Mother's Day and visited again on Tuesday, which was my regular day off from work at Stop & Shop. By Wednesday night, my sister Kathy, who was a nurse, called me at work to tell me it might be worse than we originally thought. I took Thursday off and went to the hospital. The doctor came in to talk to us about tests they wanted to do. I went back the next day to hear them tell us about a mass on her lung. She could barely come off the breathing machine to eat meals. Kelly and Michael came down from Boston to see Mom that weekend. Patti and I were discussing going to Queen of Peace to play cards or watch a Mets game when Mom went back, but as the week progressed, we realized Mom may not be going back.

I was crying outside her room in the hallway one night when one of the nurses suggested I go sit in the chapel at the end of the hall. As I entered the chapel, I felt a sacred energy. I walked slowly to the front of the chapel and found a seat in the first pew. I began to breathe very slowly and looked at a stained-glass window of the Virgin Mary. I said a Hail Mary and then began praying to Mary. I felt a calmness come over me, serenity and presence. I asked for the strength to handle whatever was about to happen. I was remembering the joy on her face and how she bolted up in the bed the previous Saturday when my son arrived. She sat straight up and exclaimed, "My boy!" with an energy and excitement she hadn't exhibited all week. I remembered how my daughter Kelly was sitting in a chair on the side of Mom's bed and how when she went to get up, my mother motioned for her to sit back down. I was also remembering how she loved the chocolate pudding they brought for dessert. The day before we asked them to bring an extra pudding. As I was feeding her the first one, she was gasping a little, so I stopped at the end of the first pudding and put the mask back on her. She suddenly motioned to the other pudding and we all laughed. Gasping or not, she wanted her second pudding, dammit. I finished my prayer and left the chapel feeling a little bit more at peace.

I was the only one in the room with her the next day when she looked at me with these pleading eyes and said, "I am scared."

I said, "What are you scared of?"

She said, "I feel like I am dying."

I said, "We are here with you, we are not leaving."

I could neither confirm nor deny so I just said we are here with you. At that point, Patti walked in the room and my mother said nothing more about it. We asked the nurse if Patti and I could stay the night and they graciously allowed us to stay. It was Wednesday, May 19th. Mom was uncomfortable all night and kept saying, "Help me."

Patti or I would rub her arm and tell her we were there. None of us slept a wink the whole night. She kept asking when she was going back to Queen of Peace, but her legs and arms were continuing to swell, so we knew it was only a matter of time. In the morning when the doctor came, we asked if we could take her back to Queen of Peace. He arranged for us to take her back on Friday by ambulance. The social worker told us, "I just want to make sure you understand that after she is taken off the machine, she may not make it back to Queen of Peace in the ambulance."

We replied, "That will be God's Will. We know she wants to go back to Queen of Peace."

On Friday morning, the social worker came back to us and said she arranged for a portable breathing machine to go in the ambulance with her. Patti accompanied Mom in the ambulance and I drove with a friend. We made it back to Queen of Peace and were greeted at the door by a group of nuns that might as well have been wearing angel wings. We got her settled in her room and we all prayed Hail Mary's around her bed, then the nuns left us alone with her.

There were a few moments of levity in those final moments. Mom asked if she could go to play bingo, which elicited a chuckle through the tears. Then the priest came to give her last rites. He was an older gentleman. When he asked us her name, we said, "Mae," but when he said the rites he called her, "Mike."

Patti and I both yelled in alarm, "Mae, Mae!"

After the priest left, the three of us sat quietly, Patti and I just listening to her breathe and watching her intently. I have never been so present in the moment. Nothing else existed for those moments. When I briefly looked up from her bed, I saw an American flag flying right outside the window and the sun was shining brightly. I don't even know why, but Patti began to sing "Silent Night" and I joined her. When my mother stayed at my house for Christmas Eve, we would attend midnight Mass and her favorite part was when they turned down the lights down after communion and we sang "Silent Night" before just sitting there in silence:

Silent night,

Holy night,

All is calm,

All is bright,

Round yon virgin,

Mother and child,

Holy infant, so tender and mild,

Sleep in heavenly peace,

Sleep in heavenly peace.

Suddenly, the blinds on the window began blowing in the wind making lots of noise. At first, I thought it was her spirit leaving, but then the blinds stopped, and my mom, eyes closed, had the biggest smile on her face, grinning from ear to ear. Then she took a last gasp and became still, and the blinds began fluttering again. Mom took her last breath May 21, 2010 at 3pm.

My sister's friend had already gone to get the nuns. They came, felt her pulse, and pronounced her gone. We all began praying around the bed again. Then we stopped, and they told some stories about her. We shared laughter and love. It was one of the most significant experiences of my life. I was so grateful to be able to escort my mom from this world to the next. I appreciate and miss her more and more each day. I am grateful I was able to tell her one Thanksgiving how grateful I was for her. I said, "I am the mother I am because of you."

When I was younger, I wished she guided us more, I wanted more structure and discipline. But because of her, I knew my kids were capable of things at a young age because I was capable. That is what made me allow them to make decisions for themselves at an earlier age. I remember how surprised and happy she was that I said that.

I am also grateful I gave her the gift of her first granddaughter and grandson. I never saw her so happy. I gave her a sweatshirt that said, "If I knew being a grandmother would be this much fun, I would have had them first!"

My son, Michael, delivered a beautiful, heartfelt and meaningful eulogy at her funeral mass. Kelly did a reading from the altar and stood with her younger cousin, Shannon, to support her while Shannon did a reading. We had an amazing singer come to sing "Ave Maria." Every time we were at a wedding or funeral and heard "Ave Maria," my mother would turn to us and say, "I want this sung at my funeral."

We would all roll our eyes and say, "OK, MOM."

Now that the time had come, we were grateful that my dear friend Patty's daughter-in-law, who sang at church and had a magnificent voice, had agreed to sing "Ave Maria." I sobbed through the entire song. She did a magnificent job and I could not stop thinking about how important this was to my mom. She didn't ask for much, but always, always mentioned this request. I knew she was smiling down on us. The beautiful song, "her boy" doing the eulogy, and her two granddaughters doing the readings. I am so grateful all this was possible.

I am so grateful that Patti and I were with her as she transitioned. One hand on her shoulder, one hand on her arm, hearts and breath connected, we escorted her from this world to the next.

I am so grateful.

Chapter 3: Small Steps Lead to Big Success

"The journey of a thousand miles begins with a single step." - Lao Tzu

***

On a cool November morning just a few months after my 39th birthday, I stared at myself in the full-length mirror in my bedroom. I was trying to button a red blazer, size 14, that my mother-in-law had given to me when I gained some weight during my pregnancy. I normally wore size 8, but I needed something larger just temporarily, or so I thought. But there I was, eight years later, trying and failing to button the largest size blazer in my closet. I felt completely overwhelmed, knowing full well that I would not be able to fit into this blazer that season. Devastation set in as I looked in the mirror and thought, "How did I ever get here?"

Shortly thereafter, I joined Weight Watchers and took my first small step on a long journey. I eventually lost fifty-two pounds and decided to become a Weight Watchers leader to support others in losing their weight, too.

I started wearing small sneakers around my neck at my meetings (and I still do at my workshops today) as an anchor and reminder that small steps lead to big success and developed the following formula to inspire others to reach their goals.

Find Support: Seek out the people, places and things that propel you closer to your goal.

Take Small Steps: Break down your goals to make them more manageable and avoid feeling overwhelmed.

Move Towards What You Want: Instead of moving away from what you don't want. Avoid resistance, deprivation and suffering. Attitude is everything.

***

Find Support

The same day that I struggled to fit into the red blazer, I was talking to my friend Maureen on the phone. I told her how frustrated I was and said, "I do not want to turn forty this summer and be fat and forty. I am starting to think maybe I want to join Weight Watchers."

Maureen said, "Yes, I was thinking about joining." She was also turning forty and feeling the same way.

I said, "Let's do it, let's go tomorrow."

The next day we joined Weight Watchers and attended our first meeting at a center in my town. Neither of us liked the leader of the meeting. We just did not connect with her at all, but we still wanted to lose the weight, so we decided to check out other meetings. The next week we went to a different center about fifteen minutes from my house. Within ten minutes of the meeting starting, I knew I liked the leader, Maggie. She seemed kind, had a sense of humor, and made the meeting FUN. We began attending her meeting each week. She liked to mingle in the lobby before the meeting, writing out name tags and asking everybody how their week had been or if we had any questions, challenges or celebrations. Once the meeting started, Maggie became animated and enthusiastic. She clearly loved her job. Her eyes sparkled, and she broke into a big smile as she emphatically pointed out that she had lost 72 ½ pounds. That last half pound was a particular point of pride. She loved to engage and entertain the crowd. When she told a story, you felt like you were right there with her.

One day she entered the meeting, wearing a suit with little plastic snack bags attached. One of them contained pretzels, another had M&M's, another had a few potato chips, one had a cookie, and another contained Hershey's Kisses. The flip chart in the front of the room read "BLT." Members began to question what the bags were, to which she replied, "Oh, this? This is nothing, it's a few pretzels, a handful of M&M's. Oh, this? Maybe a few chocolate kisses, just some potato chips." Then she asked someone to look up the points for her little bags, which turned out be much higher in calories than you might think. She revealed that BLT stood for the bites, licks and tastes that we thought were nothing but could really add up and sabotage our weight loss efforts.

Maggie was definitely a big reason I stuck with Weight Watchers and joining with a friend made it that much easier. Maureen and I attended meetings together, shared recipes, and provided moral support for each other. Our regular meeting was on Wednesday mornings, but about six months in, Maggie was promoted to a training position and stopped doing all her meetings except Monday nights. I worked on Monday nights, so I could not switch and continued attending on Wednesday morning with a new leader named Susan. She had a different style than Maggie, but I still enjoyed her meetings because she always had something profound to share and focused more on what was going on in the head than the food on the plate. When I was about six pounds away from my goal weight, I happened to have two Mondays off from work, so I decided to attend Maggie's next two meetings. Maureen and I attended the first Monday together, but she couldn't make the following Monday. She jokingly warned me, "Don't get to goal tonight!"

I told her, "Don't worry, I still have 4.8 pounds to go."

I arrived about fifteen minutes before the meeting started and felt a tingle of excitement as I stepped on the scale. I expected that I had only lost a pound or two, so I was stunned when the receptionist exclaimed, "Down 4.8, you hit goal!"

I squealed, "What?! Are you kidding me?!"

My first thought was, "Maureen's never gonna believe this."

My next thought was, "Everything happens for a reason. I can't believe Maggie is going to be the one to celebrate reaching goal with me and present me with my goal star."

It was only fitting, because I never would have reached goal if I hadn't been so motivated from her meeting the week before. My hands trembled, and my heart pounded as Maggie called me to the front of the room to receive my star. I felt so grateful to share my accomplishment with her. For the rest of the night, I was so thrilled I could barely contain myself. I felt I was finally back in control of my life. I was two months shy of my 40th birthday and instead of being Fat and Forty, I would be Fit and Forty. My clothes fit me, I had more energy, my blood glucose was controlled, and I needed less insulin. Mission accomplished. I decided to help others achieve the same success by becoming a Weight Watchers Leader myself.

I worked as a receptionist for a year and then attended leader training. I worked with a mentor (Susan, the leader who replaced Maggie at my regular Wednesday meetings) and led parts of Susan's Tuesday morning meeting at a center in Lynbrook. After four weeks, Susan had a planned day off and chose me to fill in for her and run the full meeting on my own for the very first time. As her members arrived, I overheard a few of them ask, "Where's Susan?" with a look of disappointment on their faces. My heart began to beat faster. As luck would have it, Maggie was there to observe me and provide feedback on my performance. She noticed that I seemed nervous and came over to me just before the meeting started. She looked me right in the eyes and exclaimed, "Just have fun!"

That was just the encouragement I needed. I took a deep breath and thought, "Be yourself, you are prepared." The meeting went off without a hitch; but I did question whether I allowed the members to go off on a tangent about food choices and recipes for too long. After the meeting, Maggie excitedly approached me to give her feedback. She said, "The meeting was fun. The members were engaged. I loved the way you did celebrations and so skillfully moved from members talking about products from the supermarket to the topic at hand." I felt like I was walking on a cloud.

About a year after that, Maureen reached her goal weight. She said the first two years she was getting ready, and then it only took her a year. She had been attending a meeting led by a leader named Patty, who became one of my closest friends from Weight Watchers. I attended the meeting myself the week that I thought she would reach goal. Patty allowed me to present Maureen with her goal star. Before doing so, I presented her with a thick rope toy for a dog and told a story about the weight loss journey. I said, "Losing weight is like a tug of war. Sometimes you are making great choices, and you feel in control. Everything is going great, and you feel like you are winning. Then, sometimes you aren't making great choices, and you feel like you are being pulled in the other direction. Sometimes you feel like you are being dragged into the mud, but the most important thing is that you don't let go of the rope. Maureen never let go of the rope, so I now have the privilege to give her this rope toy as an anchor, a reminder to never let go of the rope."

***

F
U
N

I have always loved acronyms. Part of my signature style used at Weight Watchers involved a blank flip chart with the letters, FUN, written vertically. The F and the U depended on the topic. For example, **F** could be:

Follow your heart
Find recipes
Feel empowered
Fit and **Fabulous**
U could be:
Understand the benefits
Use positive self-talk
Unleash your creativity
Uplift your spirit
N always represented **Nurture yourself**.

My biggest lesson during my weight loss journey was the necessity of self-care. I enjoyed walking in nature, which quickly became a daily habit. I didn't even realize how valuable my walks were until one day when I did not get my daily walk in. I was a little impatient, and my son commented, "You didn't walk today, did you?" Not only did my walks benefit me, but they also benefited my whole family. I was happier, healthier and more patient when I took care of myself.

To accomplish my weight loss goal, I knew that I would need to have more patience. Maggie helped me focus this goal using a tool called anchoring. She asked me to think of a time when I had patience and imagine it as vividly as possible. I immediately thought of a moment shortly after my babies, Kelly and Michael, were born. I was sitting in the intensive care nursery. I could hear the beeping of the monitors, the movement of the nurses all around me, and the wonderful scent of newborn babies. I felt a sense of calm, a sense of patience and purpose. Then Maggie told me to connect this feeling to a gesture, photograph, or object that I could use as an anchor. I connected the feeling to one of my most treasured photos, showing Kelly and Michael lying together in a bassinet wrapped in pink and blue blankets.

After becoming a leader myself, I celebrated my first year at goal by combining my love of acronyms and the anchoring tool by holding up a can of PAM cooking spray to help explain my success:

Positive Attitude

Activity - Walking, Yoga, Dancing

Music - Lifting Me Up & Calming Me Down

Yes, I really do love acronyms.

As I stood in front of the room supporting, empowering, inspiring and giving hope to others, I knew I had discovered my purpose. A friend had recently asked me, "What do you do at the meetings?"

My immediate response was, "I give hope."

I heard the words "I give hope" before I even thought about my answer. I wondered, "Is this what so passionately drives me? To give hope because I thought my father was hopeless?" Yes, indeed it was.

As the Scottish theologian William Barclay once said, "There are two great days in a person's life-- the day we are born and the day we discover why."

***

Small Steps

The night before I joined Weight Watchers, our family adopted a dog from the North Shore Animal League and named him Pepper. I began joining my children after school on a ten-minute walk around the block with the dog. Then I started walking with a group of mothers at the park after the kids got on the school bus. We were always chatting so didn't even realize how far we had walked. By the time I lost fifty-two pounds, I was walking four miles every day.

One day I received a flyer in the mail that promoted joining a marathon team to raise money for cancer research. I stood in the kitchen and thought, "Should I do this?" What really surprised me was that I believed I could do it. I knew I was capable of great things. Just a few years earlier, I saw a magazine called *Marathons* at one of my friends' houses and thought, "What kind of a person does a marathon?" Apparently, now I was the type of person to do a marathon.

The day after receiving the first flyer, I received a different flyer to join Team Diabetes in Bermuda for a Walking Marathon. As someone who had lived with diabetes for twenty-nine years, I felt compelled to respond. I knew this was my marathon. I began fundraising and working with a trainer, Nancy. One small glorious step at a time. I felt awesome. I started by walking four to six miles daily and doing one long walk each week, starting with ten miles then taking the next day off. I added two more miles to the long walk each week.

Besides mileage training, I had to be very careful calculating proper nutrition and managing healthy blood sugar numbers for my diabetes. Activity burns sugar, so I had to experiment how much to eat and how much insulin to take, which varied depending on how long I walked. I kept detailed records so I could manage the 26.2-mile walk.

When I got to eighteen miles, I did the walk with a friend, Cyndi. Afterward, we both collapsed into the grass and looked up at the big beautiful blue sky, feeling completely wiped out. I went home and spent the rest of the day in a hammock in my backyard still looking up at that big beautiful blue sky, feeling content and imagining all the possibilities that the future now held. After that, the mileage seemed easy: twenty, then twenty-two, then twenty-four. The one mistake I made was getting a new pair of sneakers right before the twenty-four-mile day. Yes, you guessed it--I developed big blisters on the heels of my feet. One was so big that I had to cut the back off my sneaker just to finish the training. But I was determined, nothing was going to stop me at that point. I completed the training and raised over $3500 for diabetes research. I was ready. Even if I had to wear the sneaker with the back cut out of it, I would have.

Luckily, Judy and Janet, two nurses that attended my Weight Watchers meetings, gave me cushioned, medicated pads to wear the last week of training and for the marathon. The blisters healed nicely that week, so I was able to wear my normal sneakers. I felt so grateful for that.

A few weeks before the marathon, John Hanc, a writer for a local newspaper called *Newsday*, interviewed Team Diabetes while his photographer snapped several photos of us training and a few of me using my insulin pump. On the day that our story was published, my husband arrived home, copy in hand, and said with a grin, "Wait till you see this." I opened to the cover of the Fashion & Fitness section to see Nancy and the four members of Team Diabetes walking across a little bridge in a park in Massapequa. The headline read, "WALK But Don't Run: Four Long Islanders from Team Diabetes take steps for a cause by joining the first-ever slow-paced marathon in Bermuda." Ah, how exciting! I thought there would be a small blurb about us, but I never dreamed we would be featured as the cover story. One of the photos of me holding my insulin pump even made it into the story. To this day, I keep a framed copy of that cover in my home office.

But not everything was sunshine and rainbows. During this time, my husband and I had been going through some marital problems. Right up until the day I left for Bermuda, there was tension between us and our relationship had become very strained. I didn't even want him to take me to the airport, so my friend Joann drove me instead. I met my trainer Nancy and the rest of Team Diabetes at the airport. I felt so excited to actually be completing a marathon. When I first decided to join Team Diabetes, I read that only 1% of the population ever completes a marathon in their lifetime. I also felt a little nervous about flying just two months after 9/11, but there was nothing that could stop me now.

When the plane finally touched down in Bermuda, I exhaled in appreciation of arriving safe and sound. After checking into The Fairmont Southampton Princess Hotel, I walked through town with one of the other walkers purchasing some mementos to bring back for my family: an angel ornament for my daughter and Bermuda t-shirts for my son and my husband. The excitement built as we ate lunch in a cute little restaurant and admired all the colorful buildings.

The real fun began when we went to the Expo at the Hamilton Princess Hotel a few blocks away. We received an info packet, a red Team Diabetes tank top to wear for the race and a race bib. The next day, we went to the beach and relaxed before the following day's race. That night, we ate a big pasta dinner to build up our carbs in anticipation of the race in the morning. Despite my excitement and enthusiasm about the race, I got a good night's sleep and awoke Sunday morning to some clouds and mist in the air, great weather for a long walk. I applied some sunscreen anyway, but I felt grateful it would not be a strong sun day since I burn so easily.

I wore a belt around my waist that held two bottles of water, lots of raisins, a peanut butter and jelly sandwich, and my blood tester. I intended to drink water at every station and not stop to use the bathroom unless absolutely necessary. I also wore a pair of headphones so I could play a cassette tape (I know, I'm dating myself) with all my favorite songs to keep me motivated along the road.

As we lined up at the starting point, my heart began to beat faster and faster. The excitement in the air was palpable. A British Officer in ceremonial dress blew a horn to signify the start of the marathon. I loved the ritual. Everything felt so special.

And then we were off. I felt strong, confident and capable. Joe, the Team Diabetes pacer, rode alongside our team on a bicycle offering words of support and encouragement. The picturesque route offered views of the crystal-clear water along one side and colorful houses and buildings on the other side with beautiful flowers throughout the course. If you are going to walk 26.2 miles, Bermuda is a great place to do it.

Nancy told us before the race to "pace yourself, don't start too fast or you will run out of steam," so I tried to keep a steady pace. I had to test my blood occasionally, because I had suspended my pump and was not receiving any insulin. At the halfway mark, I ate my peanut butter and jelly sandwich. I was feeling strong and the music was awesome. At the 24-mile marker, I began to tire, but my spirits were lifted when "Ain't No Stoppin' Us Now" by McFadden and Whitehead came on my playlist. Ah, just what I needed. I started singing and moving faster. At the 25-mile marker, along came Joe to walk me in the last mile. As I crossed that finish line and they placed the medal around my neck, I experienced a feeling of exhilaration like never before. Prior to the race, I targeted an average pace of 15 minutes per mile, so I was thrilled to find out that I had finished with an overall pace of 13.5 minutes per mile.

Joe encouraged us all to go to the beach and jump in the cold water after the race to help our muscles recover. He was a massage therapist, so we followed his advice. Oh, did that water feel fabulous! As I swam around, I gazed upward at the big beautiful blue sky again, feeling content, proud and certain that the future held great possibilities.

Completing that marathon meant so much to me for so many reasons: raising money for diabetes research, being part of an amazing supportive team, receiving support from family, friends, neighbors, and colleagues with donations, and the ability to train and actually walk 26.2 miles. I felt proud to be called an athlete at the celebration dinner the night of the race. I am an athlete! What a memorable experience it was for me. Small steps did lead to Big Success.

***

Move Towards What You Want

While training for the marathon, I realized that I had been stuffing my feelings with food rather than confronting the real issues in my life. After losing all the weight and changing my lifestyle, I decided it was time to train to use an insulin pump instead of taking four daily injections, one at each meal and one at bedtime. Using a pump meant changing the infusion site/needle every three days instead of having to carry my insulin and supplies with me and take four daily injections. This created quite a bit more freedom. After making all these changes in my lifestyle, there was one more major change that I knew I had to make: I could no longer pretend that I was happy in my marriage.

Since my husband and I were only a few months away from our 20th wedding anniversary, I wasn't prepared to confront him about it yet, but I knew I had to face the elephant in the room eventually. Our deteriorating relationship had become a roadblock to me being my authentic self. Ending my marriage was one of the most difficult decisions I have ever made, just excruciatingly painful. I knew it wasn't working, he knew it wasn't working too, but just like the Gladys Knight song, neither of us wanted to be the first to say goodbye.

There are two sides to every story and both of us bear some responsibility for the end of our marriage. I am aware of that now; however, that's not how I felt at the time. Although Mike kept saying that he wanted to be married, I felt he was not participating in the marriage. He reminded me of a baseball player who kept saying he wanted to play in the game but stayed in the dugout. I wanted support but didn't feel that I was getting it from him.

I spent hours laboring over this decision, but in the final analysis, I kept coming back to a poem my grandfather had sent to my mother called, "Children Learn What They Live", and that title stuck with me. Children do learn what they live. I've always felt that actions speak louder than words. It doesn't matter what I say, it is more important what I do. I knew I was not happy, so what could I possibly be portraying to my children?

After my weight loss journey, I felt healthier, more present and much more aware of my feelings. Even more than that, I felt empowered. I was no longer willing to pretend. I framed the William Shakespeare quotation, "Above all else, to thine own self be true".

One day as my husband and I walked along the boardwalk at Jones Beach, I finally built up the nerve to express my frustration and pleaded with him to go to marriage counseling. I was still trying to save the marriage at that point. Mike told me that all he needed was me, he didn't need counseling. Ultimately, he refused to go.

About four months after that first conversation, we walked along the boardwalk once again, but this time I was no longer trying to save the marriage and I told him that I thought we should separate. We sat in the car together and cried, both of us saying that we never thought we would be here. I dreaded the next part: telling all our family members.

The first person I shared the news with was my sister, Patti. She knew that Mike and I had been having problems, so she was not quite as surprised as I suspected the rest of the family would be and offered me the support I needed at that time.

Next up was my mother. I was extremely anxious about telling her because she adored Mike and I knew this would be a shock to her. Everyone thought we were such a happy family. I slept at Patti's house in Brooklyn one night and decided that on my way home to East Meadow I would stop in Whitestone to tell my mom. As Patti and I talked about it, my neck and shoulders grew tighter and tighter. I was amazed how my thoughts were creating such a physical response. As the tension built, Patti offered to tell my mother for me. I said, "No, this is my responsibility. I have to have this conversation with her."

After I arrived at my mother's house, we sat around her kitchen table and I agonized over what I was about to say. I breathed deeply, telling her that I had something important to tell her. I felt completely uncomfortable and I was visibly upset, sweat dripping from my brow, when suddenly she bursts out, "I know, Patti told me." I think she was attempting to spare me the pain of having to tell her. She just could not bear watching me feel such pain and wanted to support me. At first, I felt angry with Patti and betrayed by her. In retrospect, I realize that she was just trying to help. It probably made it easier on my mother, too. But that anticipation of telling my mother was just as difficult as telling my kids.

So difficult that I almost chickened out on the night that I planned to tell them. As I sat at my kitchen table, thinking, "How can I do this? Maybe not tonight," I received an encouraging email from my friend, Donna, who walked with me on Saturday mornings and knew that I was planning on speaking to Kelly and Michael that night. She told me that I'd feel better once I did it and I knew I had to have the conversation.

When I began to speak to them, Michael interrupted me, "I know you are getting DIVORCED!" The word divorce sounded so harsh and startled me. I had not fully accepted it myself. Kelly was also upset and asked if we could we go for counseling, but I told her it was too late for that. I knew I was making the right decision for everybody, but my heart broke in that moment.

The last person I knew I needed to have a conversation with was my mother-in-law Ann, with whom I had a wonderful relationship. She already knew that Mike and I were separating, but I still felt uncomfortable because I worried that I had disappointed her by choosing to divorce her son and feared it would affect our relationship.

She said, "I am not worried about you and Mike, you will be okay, but I am worried about the kids". Although I was tense about even telling her, I was relieved that she understood.

I replied, "Yes, I believe the most important thing we can do is remain united and a close family. Please help us do that."

This was new territory for us all, but especially for Mike and me. We needed to figure out how to be separated yet together. We had two children to parent together. For the most part, Mike and I always put their needs first. Mike is a great father and we kept the focus on the kids.

There were ups and downs, it was not easy for anyone.

I was on shaky ground as it was, I needed support. I was so unhappy and so sure that I was making the correct decision. I took a very long time to make this decision. I realized my support was not going to come from those closest to me because it shook their worlds too. I found myself spending more time with people who were not part of my married life, such as Nancy, my marathon coach, Cyndi, who trained me on my insulin pump, and friends from Weight Watchers where I was working. I also began going to yoga four times a week. All these people and places helped support me during one of the most challenging times of my life. Divorce is so so difficult, like a death without the wake or funeral, without feeling support, comfort and compassion from family and friends.

The two people that really supported me most during this time were Janice, my yoga teacher, and Jo Ann, a nurse I met while leading Weight Watchers meetings at Winthrop Hospital, who was also going through a divorce.

It was so wonderful to have someone going through the exact same thing you are. We understood each other and offered encouragement. We shared many tears, trials and triumphs.

When it was all over, we celebrated with a trip to Turks and Caicos. The turquoise water and gorgeous beaches were the perfect setting for my extended morning walks. I felt relieved, excited and empowered.

Because I was the one who initiated the divorce, I harbored some guilt and self-doubt while my kids were still in high school, but I finally gained a sense of closure while visiting Kelly and Michael at Boston University when they were in college. They both told me that they thought we were all better off because of the divorce. I felt so relieved and thought, "Mission accomplished." Hearing those words from my kids after many years of pain and struggle, I finally knew for certain that I had made the right decision for us all.

***

Find Support, Take Small Steps, Move Towards What You Want. So, what can you use this formula to help you tackle? Weight loss, divorce, job transitions, empty nest syndrome, selling a house, starting a business, moving to a new place, handling health challenges, just to name a few.

Find Support: seek out people, places and things that propel you closer to your goal. When I was overweight and overwhelmed, I found support in my friend, Maureen, who joined Weight Watchers with me; Maggie, the FUN leader; the weekly meetings; the group of mothers that walked with me; the new cookbook I was using to prepare delicious healthy meals; and the music I listened to to keep me going.

When I was going through my divorce, I found support in new friends, yoga and walking.

When I did my marathon I received support from my trainer, Nancy, who set my training schedule weekly, set up walks for our group, and shared stories of her experiences with races she had participated in; Team Diabetes, who gave us materials and info about fundraising and their representative, Jenn, who was there to encourage and inspire us every step of the way; Cyndi, who trained me to use an insulin pump, and actually did some training walks with me; the nurses who offered the medicated pads to wear on my blisters; and my wonderful children, who made cards to encourage me and for whom I wanted to set a good example.

Small steps lead to big success. This has been my mantra since 1997 when I began my weight loss journey. I began wearing baby sneakers around my neck at my meetings. I tied one end of a shoelace to one sneaker and then the other side to the other sneaker. I wore them around my neck as an anchor to remind others and myself that small steps lead to big success. After I left Weight Watchers and started my own business, I thought, "I need new shoes, new energy." The following week someone gave me sneaker keychains with butterflies on them. How fitting! I had recently started to use a butterfly as the logo for my business. They were perfect.

My pregnancy started with the small step of meeting with my OB-GYN to get a referral for an endocrinologist who would work closely with him during my pregnancy, my weight loss journey began with the small step of joining Weight Watchers, my marathon journey began with the small step of signing up with Team Diabetes, my divorce started with the small step of a walk on the boardwalk, selling my house started with the small step of hiring a real estate agent. And of course, each continued with more and more steps.

Taking action is the most important thing. Each small step leads us to the next step. Taking that small step shifts something. It all seems much more manageable. Looking at the big picture can sometimes be overwhelming.

I like to think what is my most important next step and continue from there.

I believe something is better than nothing. Instead of giving up, just do something, no matter how small. Breaking things down into small steps can make anything possible and lead to big success.

Move towards what you want instead of away from what you don't want. Avoid resistance, deprivation and suffering. Attitude is everything. This is my third step to success. Keep your eye on the prize.

When I was pregnant I kept my eye on two healthy babies, not the challenges or risks. Of course, I was aware of them, but my focus remained on two healthy, beautiful bundles of joy. Whatever we focus on grows. Joy creates a higher vibration.

When I was losing my weight, I kept my eye on goal weight--fit, fabulous and forty.

When I was training for my Walking Marathon with Team Diabetes, I kept my eye on crossing the finish line and donating money to diabetes research.

When I was getting divorced, I kept my eye on a happy, united family.
Find Support.
Take Small Steps.
Move Towards What You Want.

Chapter 4: You Bring Me Joy

"If one advances confidently in the direction of one's dreams, and endeavors to live the life which one has imagined, one will meet with a success unexpected in common hours." – Henry David Thoreau

***

In the years immediately following my divorce, my number one priority was maintaining a cohesive family for my children and providing them with a strong basis of faith and a good education. Therefore, I made the decision to do whatever I had to do to keep them enrolled--and more importantly, keep them challenged!--at Kellenberg Memorial High School, a Catholic school on Long Island run by Marianist brothers. To achieve this goal, I knew I had to make some sacrifices. In October 2004, I left my full-time job at Weight Watchers to take a more lucrative Customer Service Manager position at Stop & Shop so I could continue to afford my kids' tuition. I still led one meeting per week with my most loyal members because I firmly believed that empowering others to create positive change was my calling. This was my way of keeping one foot in both worlds.

I'm proud to say that Kelly and Michael graduated from Kellenberg in June 2007 and were off to Boston University in the Fall to start the next chapters in their stories. In September, my ex-husband and I packed up our cars and moved them up to Boston together. After the cars were unloaded and it was time to say goodbye, I left Kelly and her father in her dorm room where he was still finishing connecting stereo cables so she could listen to music. As I pulled out of the Warren Towers parking garage and on to Commonwealth Avenue to begin the journey back home to New York, I pressed play on my CD player and the first song to come on was "Stop Your Sobbing" by the Pretenders. I laughed through tears at the irony and smiled, thinking, "Mission accomplished!", and feeling glad that Mike was still there, being a good father and taking care of Kelly.

Over the next few months, I adjusted to life at home with no kids to take care of on a daily basis. You don't realize that your heart resides outside your body until you have children and they leave the nest to take those first fledgling steps towards lives of their own. The first day home alone I felt like I had been hit by a Mack truck. I felt lonely and utterly lost. Suddenly, I had a quiet house and free time. I didn't know what to do.

Sometime in October, I came across a website called Awakening Artistry and read the line, "How one Harvard lawyer left it all to have it all," promoting the book, *This Time I Dance: Creating the Work You Love*, by career transition expert and author Tama Kieves. I was immediately hooked and knew I had to meet this woman. In December, she would be speaking at a dinner for the Boston Women's Network at a Holiday Inn just a few blocks away from where I had dropped my kids off to college just weeks earlier. I drove up to Boston and had lunch with my kids before attending the dinner and meeting Tama. Her words inspired me like never before. She was funny, smart, and so real! Over the next few months, I attended a few single day workshops she held in the New York area and began to feel more confident in myself.

In August 2008, just a week before my 50th birthday, I attended a full weekend retreat workshop called "Jumpstart Your Creativity" that she held at the Omega Institute in Rhinebeck, New York. I had the desire to create my own motivational speaking business but still felt tentative about my plans and how to begin.

I told myself, "Don't get too enthused and come back and quit your job!"

I met so many incredible spirits that weekend and had so much fun, but I could feel myself holding back. On the last morning, Tama handed out small pink birthday candles and read the dedication in her book, *This Time I Dance: Creating the Work You Love*:

> I dedicate this book to that part of myself that
> inched forward when a thousand winds blew and she
> had but one small pink birthday candle to hold up her
> wish. I now dedicate this book and my life to that
> gleaming one and the one in all of us who listens to
> the music more than the reproach of the mind—and
> who dances as if the music were boisterous enough
> for all to hear—until of course it is.

A lump grew in my throat and tears began to roll down my cheeks as I listened to her speak. I felt like I had been holding a beach ball underwater and I simply could not hold it down any longer. At that moment, I knew I had to move forward one small glorious step at a time. That little pink birthday candle that I held in my hand as Tama read her dedication changed everything. I gave myself permission to live my wildest dreams.

Tama said, "It all comes down to this: We can deny our hearts or deny our limits."

I chose to stop denying my heart and to begin denying my limits. Now, I didn't go home and quit my job (not yet, at least!), but I did make the decision during the two-hour drive home to name my new inspirational business, "You Bring Me Joy." When I got home, I ordered business cards that read:

You Bring Me Joy

Creating Positive Change

One Small Step at a Time

Focusing on the joy already present in my life, rather than harping on the pain, always allowed me to remain positive.

I had already been planning a big celebration on the weekend of my 50th birthday around the theme, "You Bring Me Joy." Now, it held an even deeper significance for me. Initially, I just wanted to invite the ten women who supported me and brought me joy throughout my forties to dinner. But as I discussed the idea with each of these women, they all added another fun element. Susan suggested we go to Jazz at Lincoln Center. Claudia floated the idea of renting a limo to drive us into the city and booking hotel rooms. Patty offered to host a pajama party following the trip into the city at her beach house on the Long Island Sound. Do you see why I love these women so much and wanted them to be there to share in my birthday celebration?

Along with the invitations I sent out, I included a blank sheet titled "50 Things That Bring Me Joy" and asked everyone to fill it out beforehand and bring it with them to the party. Making a list of fifty things that bring you joy eventually became a standard form at You Bring Me Joy.

My wonderful kids, Kelly and Michael, drove me to Patty's house on Saturday morning for the first day of the celebration and stayed for the beginning of the party. While we waited for the limo to arrive to take us into the city, I opened gifts, and everybody shared in bouts of laughter. The positive energy was absolutely infectious.

Michael leaned over to me at one point and exclaimed, "I hope I am this happy when I turn fifty!"

After the limo arrived, we took some photos with the beach as our backdrop and then piled into the back of the limo to set off towards Lincoln Center. Along the way, we played a CD with a playlist featuring songs that bring me joy that I had created for the occasion and toasted with champagne to friendship, support, and joy.

The rest of the evening was rich with laughter, memories, music, gratitude and love. I felt truly blessed.

***

In March 2009, I held the first official workshop for my new business, You Bring Me Joy. I called the workshop, "Spring Fling," and sent email invitations to a mailing list I had been building. My pitch was simple:

Ignite motivation,

Nurture yourself,

Dance joyfully into Spring,

Feel empowered,

Create positive change,

Become curator of your own contentment.

Forty people registered. As the registrations poured in, I grew more and more excited. I reinvested the money from the first few registrations to purchase a Bose iPod dock and speaker so I could play music at my events. As I walked out of the Bose store, I felt a little extra pep in my step.

I rented a small room at the Ethical Humanist Society of Long Island in Garden City. With forty people in attendance, the small room lent a sense of intimacy to the event. During the two-hour workshop, I distributed handouts to all the attendees, played songs to help illustrate my teaching points, held partner exercises as well as group interaction, and wrapped up by having each attendee decorate a rock with a message or reminder from the event to serve as an anchor. In the days following the event, I received fabulous feedback from some of the attendees, telling me how they felt inspired and empowered and were looking forward to future events. One attendee told me that I had definitely found my calling and was meant to do this. I came away from that first experience reminding myself to feel joy, be courageous, and follow my heart. When I gave myself permission to do so, I liberated myself to bring joy to others. What an incredible feeling.

I often find myself coming back to a core question from that first workshop: What brings me joy?

Kelly and Michael bring me joy.

Music brings me joy.

Movement brings me joy (walking, yoga and dancing!)

The beach brings me joy.

Laughter brings me joy.

Inspiring, empowering and giving hope to others brings me joy.

Ask yourself, "What brings me joy?" Make a list of your answers and seek out the people, places, and activities that bring you closer to that feeling.

***

On my first birthday after starting my business, my children gave me a gift that let me know I was on the right track. Michael and Kelly came into my bedroom to wake me up and my son hit play on the CD player. As the song began to play, I realized that it was Michael singing and playing guitar. Here are the lyrics:

From the moment I picked up a guitar

What an inspiration you are

When life's getting me down

I know you'll always be around, always be around

Because you bring me a joy

That words cannot express

And you are so crazy

You'll never, never rest

Happy birthday, Ma

And to many, many more

Happy birthday, Ma

And to many, many more

Happy birthday, Ma

And to many, many more

You are a shooting star

I love you for who you are

Happy birthday, Ma

I love you for who you are

And will always be

Well, it's all right, Ma

I'm only singing this song for you

Well, it's all right, Ma

I'm only singing this song for you

Because you're living proof

That dreams really do come true

It's all right, Ma

I'm only singing this song for you

I'm your only son

And I, oh I, love you

Happy birthday!

By the time the song had ended, I had tears in my eyes. When I heard the line, "Because you're living proof that dreams really do come true," I thought, "If that is what I have taught my children, I guess I have done a good job."

***

I called the second workshop for my new business, "Celebrate and Let Go", and instructed attendees to bring something to celebrate and something to let go of. I decided to hold the workshop outdoors at Jones Beach and hope for the best weather-wise. On the day of the event, it was a bit cloudy and it looked like it might rain. I told the thirty-five people registered to attend that I would email them by 3:00 pm to confirm or cancel. Since I had never held an event outside, I felt uncertain about what to do. I kept watching the weather reports. So far, no rain. Just cloudy and a little windy. As the clock ticked closer to my self-imposed 3:00 pm deadline, I opened an email and read the following quotation, "A cloudy day is no match for a sunny disposition." Well, that settles it then. I sent all attendees confirmation of the event and headed to the beach to set up!

As people arrived, I felt a refreshing breeze blow in from the ocean and felt confident in my decision. The energy of the group was so positive and uplifting. The weather had held out and we were able to joyfully share the things we were celebrating and dance on the beach. Then Tim, a yoga teacher I had hired to lead yoga on the beach, arrived and led the group in a gentle yoga session. I watched Tim extend his arms in a T position and bend his front knees into "Warrior Two" pose just as the sun began to set above his right shoulder. The scene seemed like a photo in a magazine. I experienced this intense feeling of exhilaration and thought, "Another dream come true, practicing yoga on the beach."

After Tim left, I led an inspired group of thirty-five women as we wrote the things we wanted to let go on a rock and then charged towards the water to throw the rocks in the ocean as I played the Elvis Presley song, "Please Release Me" on my Bose speaker. A group of fishermen stood at the edge of the water with fishing poles in their hands and watched us with curious amusement--they had no idea what was going on. As my group returned to our beach chairs, one of my clients, Dottie, said to me, "so where did you find thirty-five women just as crazy as you to attend?" I laughed and felt connected to all these women, feeling the joy and catharsis all around us. I received so many wonderful emails the next day telling me how the weather did not matter at all. I experienced total contentment, thinking this is what I am meant to do. I was so at ease, it just flowed.

That night, I woke up from a deep sleep with a clear revelation: it was time for me to become a yoga teacher. When I first began practicing yoga, I immediately fell in love and wanted to become a teacher, but I chastened myself: why do you always have to teach, lead, be the manager, the parent, the person in charge? Just be a student and receive. Now, eight years had passed, and I knew I was ready to give back. I sat straight up out of bed and immediately went downstairs to my computer to research Yoga teacher training at Kripalu. I knew that if I was going to train, then Kripalu was the place where I wanted to do my training.

I enrolled in the 200-hour training beginning with two weeks in November 2009 and concluding with another two weeks in the end of January 2010, graduating on Friday, February 5, 2010. This four-week training was not so much life-changing as it was life-enhancing. On day one, Jurian, one of the teachers, told us that there would be a lot of info coming at us like water flowing from a fire hydrant, so just "trust the process." Those became magical words throughout my training and beyond, just TRUST THE PROCESS.

Graduation morning began with temple sadhana--sitting across from a partner with a candle, a cup of water, and a rose petal. Sara Svati, one of the assistants, sat in the front singing a soft, beautiful, meditative melody in her angelic voice. My partner's name was Kathleen. I softly caressed her face with the rose petal, then her hands and her feet. I placed a drop of water to her third eye (the area between the eyebrows), her wrists and her feet.

After morning sadhana, we had a silent breakfast, designed to start the day in a quiet way and be more mindful of the food giving you nourishment and energy, time to commune with one's self. After breakfast, I walked outside to watch the beautiful blazing sun over the mountains. So picturesque, so magnificent, so significant, so symbolic, it was like the universe knew this was a very special day! I said to myself, "I am a yoga teacher" and tears came to my eyes. I stood there for a long moment soaking in the sun, the mountains and the gratitude. I felt so blessed.

I went back inside and gathered together with the other trainees in the hallway, where photos were taken, and hugs exchanged. We had shared an amazing journey together. As the doors opened to the Shadowbrook Room where the graduation ceremony would be held and one of our teachers, Devarshi, came out to give us final directions, tears rolled down my face. Inside, pillows and candles with ivy lined a path to the front of the room. To signify purity, the teachers and assistants all wore white. They stood at the door ringing bells, symbolic of all the angels around us.

After everyone had entered, we were each called up one by one to the start of the path by the assistants, where Abby held a candle near you and talked about the light, Sara sprinkled rice to signify abundance, Morgan tossed rose petals, and Mary, Kolbi, and Steven sprinkled water. Then you walked up the path lined on both sides by the other graduates with arms open and palms up to receive each person offering words about you as you walked. When you got to the end, Devarshi put orange oil on your third eye, passed a blessing by Swami Kripalu, looked into your eyes, used your name and said beautiful things. "Always be your authentic self, you are loving, open, humorous."

Then, Jurian placed mala beads around your neck and said, "Continue to be your wonderful, authentic self."

Danny handed you your certificate as sacred music played. Once all the graduates had received their certificates, we exchanged hugs and tearful goodbyes.

Before returning home, I drove up to Boston where both Kelly and Michael were attending Boston University so I could celebrate my graduation with them. During my training at Kripalu, I was touched by a message I received from Kelly saying, "I am so proud of you, Mama."

The ride was a bit longer than I expected but well worth the trip. I shared a delicious dinner with Kelly and Michael to celebrate my graduation from Yoga Teacher Training and spent the weekend catching up on all that was happening with them. I always loved visiting Boston while they were in school. I felt content in my own life and proud of the lives I had enabled my children to lead.

I reflected on the lessons I learned from starting my own business and becoming a certified yoga teacher. Give yourself permission to follow your heart and always remember what brings you joy. Then, when you find it, share your joy with others.

Chapter 5: The Beauty of the Butterfly

"We delight in the beauty of the butterfly but rarely admit the changes it has gone through to achieve that beauty." -Maya Angelou

***

I love butterflies. Their fluttering wings, abundance of color, their graceful movements as they dance through the air. I am inspired by the lightness of butterflies, both light of weight and light of being. Butterflies, though fragile, are resilient. Strong and beautiful. Much like the lives to which many of us aspire. It is for this reason that I chose to use a butterfly as the logo when I started my wellness coaching business.

The first time I began to associate butterflies with the process of transformational life change occurred while I was pregnant with my twins. Shortly after finding out I would be having not just one, but two babies (!!!), I felt a fluttering of movement in my belly. The only way I could describe the feeling was that of a butterfly gently flapping its wings. What a magical feeling. This intense love would begin my greatest transformation because the only way for me to feel all this love would be for me to begin lowering the walls of protection I had carefully built around myself after my father's death. To truly and fully experience such unconditional love, I had to feel the pain as well. Numbness was no longer an option. To luxuriate in the blessing, I needed to experience the struggle.

Spiritual teacher Anthony DeMello tells a story about the butterfly's transformation that goes like this:

> *"One day a man saw a butterfly shuddering on the sidewalk, locked in a seemingly hopeless struggle to free itself from it's now useless cocoon.*
>
> *Feeling pity, he took out a pocket knife and he carefully cut out and around the cocoon so that he could free the butterfly from the struggle. To his dismay, it lay on the sidewalk and convulsed weakly for a few moments and then died.*
>
> *A biologist later told him that that was the worst thing he could have done. A butterfly needs the struggle to develop the muscles to fly. By robbing him of the struggle he had made him too weak to fly."*

I decided that I would not be too weak to fly. I allowed myself to let in the feelings of pain and betrayal and abandonment I had harbored since my father's death and engaged myself fully in the act of being a mother to these two little babies. Once they were old enough for me to begin thinking about myself again and my own needs, I realized that I would never be happy as long as I was overweight. So, I committed myself to losing the weight no matter how hard it proved, and I did.

Shortly after reaching my goal weight, my sister Patti and I were shopping in Macy's. I saw a gold butterfly pin in the costume jewelry section that I really liked. Patti purchased it for me as a gift for reaching my goal weight. That solidified it for me. Butterflies were symbolic of all the transformations I had made in my life and would continue to make. I had gone from an overweight and overwhelmed caterpillar to a fit and fabulous butterfly.

As the years went on, I received many butterfly gifts. Pins, knick knacks, candles and cards. They serve as a reminder of my transformation, of the struggle and the blessing. Anna, one of the Weight Watchers members who attended my Wednesday morning meetings after I became a leader, wore a butterfly pin that I loved to one of my meetings. She collected jewelry and attended jewelry shows, so I asked her where she got it. She said she bought it at a show and that they were no longer available. Of course, months later, she gave me a wrapped box and said, "I know you like this one." When I opened the box and saw the exact pin I had asked her about, I broke into tears. The butterfly was so beautiful, blue in some parts then purple in others with light tinges of yellow and orange on the tips of its wings. I couldn't have possibly dreamt of a butterfly more stunning in its beauty. When I decided to go part-time at Weight Watchers and return to Stop & Shop full-time, I received another gift from Anna: a small box waiting for me at the front of the meeting room with a note that read,

Dear Noreen,

Another Transformation!!

Life is good.

Love,

Anna

Inside the box, I found another butterfly pin, somehow even more beautiful than the first one she had given me, with wings made of Mother of Pearl stones supporting a body made of Amethyst. I hope that Anna knows how much both gifts meant to me and how dearly I cherish both pins to this day. They both serve as another reminder of the gratitude I have for the struggles that have allowed me to receive and appreciate all the blessings in my life.

When I decided that I wanted to use a butterfly in the logo for the new business I was starting, there was only one person who came to my mind who would be able to create it for me. Her name is Norma and she has served a great many purposes in my life, from being something of a second mother to me growing up in Whitestone, Queens to becoming a client of mine after I started my own business, which only deepened the bonds of our relationship. Norma is also an incredibly gifted artist whose works of art adorned her house on 17th Road in Whitestone, the same house where her daughter Claudia and I used to come after school when we were little girls. Claudia was my best friend, so I was always going over to her house, where we would sit in the kitchen and talk about what was going on at school. I remember how Norma always sat so patiently, listening intently to whatever we were talking about. She made me feel like she cared so much. She made me feel loved.

Norma also attended Weight Watchers meetings when we were kids, so I've always associated Weight Watchers with her. She always seemed to be at the stove cooking something that smelled delicious, including one particularly memorable recipe for chicken with orange juice and soy sauce that she baked in the oven. Everyone loved it!

Even as I got older, Norma remained an important part of my life. My sister Patti and I slept at Norma's house the night before I got married. Patti, Claudia, her sister Stephanie who was the same age as Patti, and I shared so many memories and laughs as we stayed up very late that night. Norma had cookies and champagne ready for everyone the next morning, as the bridesmaids: my mother; my uncle, Gene, who was walking me down the aisle in place of my father; and his wife, Aunt Helen, arrived for photos with the photographer. Claudia's father Mike was going to sing at the church. Five years earlier, after I had just gotten my license, Mike took me to buy my first car. I did not know anything about cars and I was so grateful for the assistance. And just a few years before that, Claudia and Stephanie came and played Monopoly with me at the hospital after being diagnosed with diabetes at age 14. Norma,

Claudia and the whole Mosia family provided a bit of a cocoon for me as a child. I always felt so much love there. For this and so many other reasons, Norma has always held a very special place in my heart, which is why I felt that it would be such an honor if she would paint my butterfly.

In early 2009, Norma had been attending my weekly meetings on creating positive change for several months when I decided to ask her if she would be willing to paint a butterfly for me to use as the logo for the business, which I was calling "You Bring Me Joy" at the time. She agreed immediately and told me to pick some colors and we scheduled a time for me to come to her house to play around with color and design. In the days leading up to our meeting, I began noticing what colors were resonating with me. Green, blue and purple were my favorites, so I found some tissue paper in those colors and brought it with me to our meeting.

As the door opened to Norma's house in Whitestone, I felt transported back to 1970. The aroma of her cooking permeated the whole house. A typical Italian mother, she said, "Of course, we will have a meal first." We sat around that same kitchen table that I remembered so well from my childhood and shared a delicious, healthy meal of oven baked fish, sweet potatoes, and broccoli. Norma put so much love into her cooking that you could taste it. When I cook broccoli and sweet potatoes, it never tastes as wonderful as when Norma does. After lunch, we moved to her paint studio. I enjoyed watching her come so alive as we played with different paint colors. I had never witnessed her in this arena before. She was so passionate, so excited and so lit up. We decided on the exact colors and agreed she would play around with a few ideas and paint several butterflies over the next week that I could decide from. The following week she gave me seven designs, but I immediately knew which one I wanted. The butterfly that I have used for nearly ten years and still use as my logo to this day. Symbolizing transformation, the colors represent the following chakras (which I did not know about at the time but have since learned): Green for the 4th chakra, the heart; Blue for the 5th chakra, the throat; and Purple for the 6th chakra, the 3rd eye, or intuition. Open your heart, speak your truth and trust your intuition, your inner knowing. These have been my most important lessons in life and at the root of all I teach, yet these colors came together so effortlessly and serendipitously. I believe you can only truly stand in your power through love, authenticity, and trust, qualities that I invested in my relationship with Norma, which resulted in a butterfly born with so much personal significance. My butterfly. Thank you, Norma.

A few years later, I was on my way home from Kripalu after graduating from Let Your Yoga Dance teacher training when I felt compelled to stop at Norma's house in Whitestone. The ride from Kripalu to my home in Floral Park was about three hours, but luckily, Whitestone was along the way. The further I drove, the stronger the feeling grew. I pulled up in front of her house and saw a light on, so I called Norma from my cell phone.

"Hi Norma, it is Noreen."

"Oh my goodness, I have goosebumps. I have been thinking about calling you for the last few days. I want help on my weight loss journey."

"Well, I am outside your house right now."

"Come in, come in!"

I went in and we sat around that familiar kitchen table once again. We talked for hours and I agreed to come over on Wednesdays. I would weigh her, we would have a delicious lunch she had prepared, and I would coach her. We began to have the most amazing conversations. One day as I sat there at her kitchen table, I thought, "Wow, when I was ten years old, I would sit here, and she would listen intently. Now, forty-five years later, there I was, sitting and listening intently to HER." Because I visited weekly, we shared so much and grew even closer. She framed the other six butterflies she had painted and gave them to me to hang in my apartment, where they still hang today. She lost twenty pounds during the first year and helped me make important decisions about my business. First, she provided the cocoon to protect me while I struggled, then she painted my butterfly, then she gave me the most wonderful gift of all: the opportunity for me to repay the favor and help her with her own transformation.

You must delight in the beauty of the butterfly while also acknowledging the changes it has gone through to achieve that beauty. With age and experience, I have learned to appreciate the blessing in the struggle. And there's almost always a struggle. It is precisely that which makes the blessing so wonderful and so worthy of gratitude and appreciation.

I struggled through a double high-risk pregnancy before receiving the blessing of two beautiful babies.

I struggled with my weight, becoming extremely overweight and overwhelmed, and joined Weight Watchers, struggling to lose the weight before receiving the blessing of becoming fit, forty and a Weight Watchers leader with more energy than I had in my twenties.

I struggled training for the walking marathon in Bermuda before receiving the blessing of crossing the finish line, having my medal put around my neck, and donating $3400 to diabetes research.

I struggled through my divorce before receiving the blessing of a happier, healthier family with stronger relationships.

I struggled going part-time at Weight Watchers and becoming a Stop & Shop supermarket manager before receiving the blessing of seeing Kelly and Michael graduate from Kellenberg Memorial High School.

I struggled through the overwhelming process of selling the house I owned for 26 years. There was so much to pack. There were so many memories to sift through. The attic was full of clothes and toys from Kelly and Michael's childhood as well as things from my mother's house stored there. There had been so many family holidays and parties held here. The walls certainly held lots of memories. One of the last Thanksgiving/Christmas celebrations I held in the house was a celebration my kids dubbed "Thanks-Christmas-Giving" because we held a joint party in between both holidays in early December after both Kelly and Michael returned from London and Dublin respectively, where they had been studying abroad for the semester. I invited my three sisters, as well as my ex-husband Mike and his two sisters, and asked everyone to bring a dish and a memory about the house. That celebration is etched in my memory as one of the happiest ever held in that house and served as a fitting close to nearly three decades of struggle and blessings. I struggled through selling that house before receiving the blessing of financial freedom and the ability to travel.

I struggled after being diagnosed with Multiple Sclerosis before receiving the blessing of learning that my self-care really is my #1 priority. Now, I have my priorities clear:

1. My health
2. My kids
3. My bliss

I own my time, so I own my life. I am more present than ever before. I live more intentionally, I have more time and space. I am so blessed. I am so grateful.

Chapter 6: Love, Not Fear

"Our deepest fear is not that we are inadequate. Our deepest fear is that we are powerful beyond measure. It is our light, not our darkness, that most frightens us.' We ask ourselves, who am I to be brilliant, gorgeous, talented, fabulous? Actually, who are you not to be? You are a child of God. Your playing small doesn't serve the world. There's nothing enlightened about shrinking so that other people won't feel insecure around you. We are all meant to shine, as children do. We were born to make manifest the glory of God that is within us. It's not just in some of us; it's in everyone. And as we let our own light shine, we unconsciously give other people permission to do the same. As we're liberated from our own fear, our presence automatically liberates others." — Marianne Williamson

***

FEAR is:
False
Evidence
Appearing
Real

FEAR.

Fear is in our minds. Fear is how we scare ourselves, how we limit ourselves. Fear is doubt. Fear is uncertainty. Fear constricts the body and the mind.

Fear immobilizes.

LOVE is:

Life's

Only

Vital

Emotion

LOVE.

Love is in the heart. Love creates confidence. Love opens you up to all the wonderful possibilities. Love empowers. Love strengthens. Love is when you know you are exactly where you are supposed to be. Love is living on purpose.

Our lives are often characterized by the choices we make. Did we choose love? Or did we choose fear?

***

When I was in my mid-twenties, I worked as a Front End Coordinator for Pathmark Supermarkets. The role basically entailed traveling between the six stores in my region to ensure proper procedure and policy adherence. As part of my duties, I developed a quiz to help the cashiers identify different produce items that were packaged in foam trays wrapped in cellophane. One day, the Regional Produce Supervisor told me that he loved what I was doing with the cashiers and asked me if I could speak to the produce managers at their next meeting. I immediately agreed, figuring he meant the six produce managers from the six stores in my region. Later that day, I checked the work calendar and noticed that there was an all-day produce meeting at a local catering hall scheduled for the following week for all the store managers, assistant store managers, and produce managers for the entire New York area. About 200 people were expected to be in attendance. Sheer panic washed over me as I thought, "How am I going to get out of this?"

Having already agreed to do it, I couldn't come up with any reason to back out of the commitment, so I prepared my notes and came up with what I wanted to say. Eventually, the day of the meeting arrived. As I sat waiting to be called to the stage, my mind was still running through possible ways out. My palms were sweating and my heart beat faster as I thought, "Is it just me or is it a little warm in here?" I took a few deep breaths and made the decision to choose love over fear. I was prepared. I knew what I was talking about. They had asked me to speak. I could do this. I would speak slowly and just get through it.

As I walked up to the microphone, I felt hundreds of eyes staring at me and thought, "Just breathe." I focused on some familiar, friendly faces in the crowd and felt a little bit lighter. I knew I could do this. I began my remarks, speaking slowly so that I wouldn't rush through. When I get nervous, I talk too fast and feel like I seem nervous to others, which just heightens my anxiety. It's a vicious cycle. So, I spoke slowly and started to feel more comfortable until eventually I wasn't even nervous anymore. Before I knew it, I was done speaking. I practically ran off the stage and melted into a chair in the hallway with a big sigh of relief. When I asked a few of the managers later for their feedback, they all told me that I did a great job and didn't seem nervous at all. The lesson I learned that day was that you cannot give into the fear that will try to paralyze you. You must believe in yourself and take action to overcome that fear.

***

For the next decade or so, I didn't really have to speak in public for any reason so despite overcoming my fear of public speaking, I did not have the opportunity to practice that particular skill and feel more confident and capable in my ability to do so. After my twins were born, a friend referred me to a support group called the Mothers of Twins Club. The Nassau County branch had 300 members who met monthly to discuss the challenges of having twins. I joined a few months after giving birth and began attending their monthly speaker series along with different events throughout the year. After a year of attending the meetings, I decided to get more involved and co-hosted the Halloween Party along with another mother named Rita. After that went well, we both signed up to be Helping Hands, members tasked with distributing items like cribs, car seats, toys, gently used clothes, and sometimes even food to members in need. I also began to edit the monthly newsletter. After about a year of doing that, the Club approached me to join the board in the role of Vice President of Programming.

The position required setting up monthly speakers and coordinating the Installation Dinner, a ceremony in which new board members were installed for the following year, and the Holiday Dinner. I knew the Vice President would also have to run the general meeting and the board meeting in the absence of the President, but in my four years in the club that had never happened. Running those meetings was the only part of the job I was not comfortable doing, but I figured that wasn't very likely, so I accepted the position.

A month after I was installed as Vice President, the President's father passed away and I had to chair the general meeting (about 100 attending) and the board meeting (20-30 attending). Fear set in as I realized I would have to use a microphone to welcome the members, introduce each board member to come up and speak, ask for questions (never mind hoping I could answer the questions!), close the business portion of the meeting and introduce the main program. On the day of the general meeting, that old familiar feeling crept in as my palms became sweaty and my heart beat a little faster. Once again, I knew that there was no way out of the situation, so I told myself to remember to breathe and made sure to keep my water nearby throughout the program. One small glorious step at a time, I conducted the meeting, and everything went smoothly. I let out a big, big sigh of relief and shifted my focus to the board meeting the following week. That group was smaller and easier to handle. Once I got through those two meetings, I started to really feel confident, so much so that the following year I ran for President and won. Once I got past the fear, I realized I was capable of doing anything I set my mind to.

***

In October 2008, I attended Tama Kieves' workshop, "Unleash Your Calling", at Kripalu Yoga and Wellness Center in the Berkshires. I wanted to keep the energy and inspiration alive from her event I attended at Omega Institute in Rhinebeck, New York in August 2008. When I left Omega, I wrote the words, "HOLD THE VISION," on a rock as an anchor to remind me that I needed to follow my heart and hold the vision to start my own business. I even had to borrow some money from a friend to cover the cost of attending the October workshop, but I was determined and motivated to attend no matter what. This also served as a reminder that we all need a little help from our friends sometimes.

A few days into the 5-day workshop, I mustered the courage to invite Tama to join me at the noon Let Your Yoga Dance session held during the workshop's lunch break. She had other plans for that time but asked me if I could do her a favor instead. She said, "My book is *This Time I Dance,* and I have never danced at a workshop. I love your energy. Could you help me lead a dance?"

I immediately said, "YES! 'Ain't No Stopping Us Now' by McFadden & Whitehead. I have the CD in my car."

She said, "Great! Bring it back with you after lunch and you can lead the workshop in a dance."

I was so excited that I was completely caught up in the LOVE emotion. As soon as I left her, I immediately went into the FEAR emotion. What did I just volunteer for? I've never led a dance before. I don't even dance at a wedding unless I have had a drink or two. I think I have two left feet. I've never had a dance class in my life, and now I'm going to lead a dance for the 50 people attending this workshop.

Just as I'm starting to panic, I remind myself to live in the LOVE emotion and reject the FEAR emotion. Okay, just breathe... just breathe. You already said yes. Go get the CD from the car. You want to help Tama, move back into the LOVE again.

After lunch I returned with CD in hand, still feeling a little unsettled but knowing that I wanted to help Tama. I gave the CD to her assistant,

Gabriel, to queue up the song for the dance. As he begins to set it up, Tama says, "Gabriel, give Noreen a headset and mic."

As Gabriel put the headset on, I squealed, "I don't need a mic! I don't need a mic," sliding back into the FEAR again. If I didn't think I could dance, I definitely knew I could not sing. Tama and Gabriel both laughed, ignoring my protests. And then, the music began to play. The FEAR melted away. I raised my right arm up in the air and just started singing (probably off-key but who cares?) and dancing. Everyone followed my lead as I belted out the lyrics:

Ain't No Stoppin Us Now!

We're on the move!

Ain't No Stoppin Us Now!

We've got the groove!

There's been so many things that's held us down

But now it looks like things are finally coming' around

I know we've got a long, long way to go

And where we'll end up, I don't know

But we won't let nothing' hold us back

We're putting ourselves together

We're polishing up our act!

If you felt we've been held down before

I know you'll refuse to be held down anymore!

Don't you let nothing, nothing

Living In Joy

Stand in your way!

I want y'all to listen, listen

To every word I say, every word I say!

Ain't No Stoppin Us Now!

We're on the move!

Ain't No Stoppin Us Now!

We've got the groove!

Ain't No Stoppin Us Now!

We're on the move!

Ain't No Stoppin Us Now!

We've got the groove!

I know you know someone that has a negative vow

And if you're trying to make it they only push you aside

They really don't have nowhere to go

Ask them where they're going, they don't know

But we won't let nothing' hold us back

We're gonna put ourselves together

We're gonna polish up our act!

And if you've ever been held down before

I know you'll refuse to be held down anymore!

Don't you let nothing, nothing

Stand in your way!

I want y'all to listen, listen

To every word I say, every word I say!

Ain't No Stoppin Us Now!

We're on the move!

Ain't No Stoppin Us Now!

We've got the groove!

Ain't No Stoppin Us Now!

We're on the move!

Ain't No Stoppin Us Now!

We've got the groove!

When the dance was over, I had moved fully back into the LOVE again! Leading that dance was such a blast for me and Tama described it as one of the highlights of her program. One of the attendees approached me afterward and said, "Well, you couldn't really sing, but you were up there singing anyway, so I figured I could get up and dance." I decided to let that be a lesson that when you get out of your head, which represents fear, and into your body, representative of love, and just move without thinking, you empower yourself to have more fun. Once we all got moving, there really was no stopping us now!

On the last day of the program, a group of us were sitting outside talking about Halloween costumes and achieving our dreams and someone suggested that Tama and I wear "I Dream of Jeannie" costumes and be the Dream Jeannies. Tama said, "I would not do that alone, but I might do it with you."

I said, "I wouldn't do it alone either, but I would do it with you."

We all laughed, but little did they know I would take them seriously and purchase the costume when I got home. I heard that the Oprah Winfrey Show was having a contest asking viewers, "Why is 2009 going to be your best year ever?" I knew it was Tama's dream to be on Oprah, so I decided to make a video about how 2009 was going to be my best year ever because of being inspired by Tama. My ex-husband has always been good with technology, so I asked him to film it for me. We tried to shoot the video at the beach or at the park, with me wearing the "I Dream of Jeannie" costume while passersby looked on confusedly, but eventually had to settle for shooting the video in my kitchen in front of a picture of the beach due to poor weather and difficulties with sound editing. There I was, standing in my kitchen, clothed from head-to-toe in a genie costume, holding up a copy of Tama's book and talking about how 2009 would be my best year ever because of how inspired I was. We even played "Ain't No Stoppin' Us Now" and I danced around as the outro to the video. When we were finished, we couldn't help but laugh at the absurdity of it all, but I really was embracing the idea of living in the love rather than dwelling in the fear. Fear can only hold you back, whereas love can lift you up and allow you to accomplish more than you could ever possibly dream of. Ultimately, we didn't win the contest or even hear back from Oprah's team, but I think we missed the submission deadline. The contest wasn't really the point anyway. After Thanksgiving dinner that year, my family certainly enjoyed watching the video, that's for sure. I also sent a copy to Tama, who nicknamed me, "Dancing Jeannie." I liked that name. It was definitely preferable to my previous identity as the Good Little Soldier. No longer would I prioritize being the responsible one, choosing to work now and play later. Now there are benefits to being the good soldier and it has served me well at times in my life, but as with everything, there must be a balance.

Embracing the identity of the Dancing Jeannie is about living in joy. JOY empowers, ignites creativity, sparks positive energy and sustains us throughout both the trials and the triumphs.

Fast forward to January 2010 and now I'm leading my own workshop, called "Dreams, Hopes, Aspirations." I decided to wear the Dancing Jeannie costume to bring some joy to the participants and highlight the benefits of letting the love overpower the fear. I felt the fear, of course. You have to. But I told myself, "You have to come out of your comfort zone to stretch yourself and to have more fun."

I walked into the workshop wearing the Dancing Jeannie costume and holding a wine decanter that my friend Norma had painted to look like a genie bottle and the room immediately burst into laughter. I had made my point about dreams, and yes, I survived. The workshop was immensely successful and further built my confidence as I grew my inspirational consulting business.

In June 2012, I attended the second of three weeklong workshops in California as part of Jack Canfield's Train The Trainer program to become certified to teach his Success Principles. On the last night of the training, Jack held a "Come As You Are" Party, in which the attendees must behave as if it is five years into the future and you have accomplished your goal and achieved your dream. Costumes and props are encouraged, so you can probably guess what I chose to wear. Yup, I went to the party as Dancing Jeannie and brought along a mock magazine cover I had created showing me dancing on the Ellen DeGeneres Show. While I was getting dressed for the event, I began to scare myself and let the fear creep in. I had to remind myself to live in the love. Furthermore, Success Principle #15 is "Experience the fear and take action anyway." Ain't no stoppin' me now!

It felt like my heart was beating right out of my chest as I walked from my hotel room to the event space for the party. The first person I saw was Tomas, the assistant who had coached us earlier on Success Principle #15. He already knew about my history of wearing the Dancing

Jeannie costume, so his face lit up when he saw me, and he squealed in delight, "I love it!"

After that, I felt a little bit more comfortable, despite the sweat dripping from my brow betraying just how anxious I had felt up until that point. I was definitely out of my comfort zone, but people then began to run up to me, asking to take a photo with me. Dancing Jeannie was a hit once again! I felt like I had lived Success Principle #15 and stayed true to my belief in valuing the emotion of love instead of succumbing to the emotion of fear. Action alleviates anxiety.

In January 2015, nearly seven years after I first bought the costume, I attended another workshop with Tama Kieves at Kripalu. I decided that I'd surprise Tama by showing up wearing the costume. The week prior, one of my clients who had attended "Dreams, Hopes, Aspirations" brought me a Barbie doll dressed in an "I Dream of Jeannie" outfit. She said she found it amongst her things and thought of me. She said, "I still can't believe you wore that, so you should have this."

I still have that Barbie doll in a prominent place in my living room to make me smile and remind me to choose love over fear.

As I was getting dressed, I briefly doubted myself and nearly chickened out. As many times as I've worn the costume, you'd think it would get easier, but there's always that one brief moment of doubt, where I have to experience the fear and take action anyway. That's how you live in the love. So, I let myself feel the fear, then reminded myself, "You really wanted to do this. It is going to be fun. Tama is going to be so surprised. No chickening out, experience the fear and take action anyway."

So, I finished getting dressed and then, as life would have it, my room was on the third floor all the way on the other side of the building from the workshop room. I took the elevator down to the first floor, and as I walked across the building to the workshop room, I was greeted with smiles from everyone I encountered. One person asked, "Are you dancing tonight?"

To which I replied, "I am always dancing!"

When Tama arrived, she burst into laughter. It was worth every uncomfortable moment. Tama said, "If you can show up in that costume, you can do anything!"

Another attendee met me in the cafe and said, "You have a big personality, own it!"

Love, not fear.

Love empowers, love strengthens, love opens you up to all the possibilities. Love heals. Love is when you are living on purpose.

Love is when you know you are exactly where you are supposed to be.

With love, anything is possible. Anything.

LOVE.

Life's

Only

Vital

Emotion

LOVE.

Chapter 7: You Can't Be in Two Places at the Same Time

"Most obstacles melt away when we make up our minds to walk boldly through them." -Orison Swett Marden

***

Part I: You Can't Be in Two Places at the Same Time

I once heard a story about an old Cherokee chief who was teaching his grandson about life:

"A fight is going on inside me," he said to the boy. "It is a terrible fight and it is between two wolves. One is evil - he is anger, envy, sorrow, regret, greed, arrogance, self-pity, guilt, resentment, inferiority, lies, false pride, superiority, self-doubt, and ego. The other is good - he is joy, peace, love, hope, serenity, humility, kindness, benevolence, empathy, generosity, truth, compassion, and faith. This same fight is going on inside you - and inside every other person, too."

His grandson thought about it for a minute and then asked his grandfather, "Which wolf will win?"

The old chief simply replied, "The one you feed."

Positive self-talk is crucial to our success and happiness. Whatever we focus on grows. Feed the good wolf and you will feed the good parts inside yourself. Feed the evil wolf and you will only invite more negativity into your life. This choice is important because you cannot be in two places at the same time.

***

When I was a Weight Watchers leader, I was always saying, "You can't be in two places at the same time!"

You can't be beating yourself up and building yourself up at the same time. I used that line so many times that I started to say that it was going to be the name of my upcoming book. In fact, when I went to Jack Canfield's Breakthrough to Success in 2011, I made a mock book cover titled, "You Can't Be In Two Places At The Same Time," for the first Come as You Are Party I ever attended. I was trying to will the book into existence by feeding the good wolf.

At Weight Watchers, I animated the concept by slumping my shoulders and dropping my head down as I moaned, "Poor me, I can't eat anything, this is so hard, poor me."

Then I would stand tall, head held high and say, "I can, I will, small steps lead to big success."

The choice is yours.

When you are slumped over and complaining, the energy is low, but when you are standing tall and speaking positively, the energy is high. You can't be in two places at the same time. Which thoughts are you feeding?

Attitude is everything, which is why I loved sharing this quotation by Charles Swindoll at my workshops:

The longer I live, the more I realize the importance of attitude on life. Attitude, to me, is more important than facts. It is more important than the past, than education, than money, than circumstances, than failures, than successes, than what people think or say or do. It is more important than appearances, giftedness, or skill. It will make or break a company... a church... a home. The remarkable thing is we have a choice every day regarding our attitude we will embrace for that day. We cannot change our past... we cannot change the fact that people will act in a certain way. We cannot change the inevitable. The only thing we can do is play

93

on the one string we have, and that is our attitude. I am convinced that life is 10% what happens to me and 90% how I react to it. And so it is with you...we are in charge of our Attitudes.

One of my clients recently asked me, "I know you have been through many challenges--most recently, the MS diagnosis; how do you keep going?"

Without even thinking, I immediately said, "Small steps and positive self-talk." We always have a choice.

Our only power is in our choice, in how we will respond. No matter what happens or what mistakes you think you have made, what is most important is your next step. For example, if you're trying to lose weight and you eat too much ice cream, what is your next step? You could beat yourself up, feel worse about yourself, throw your hands up, give up, go into what I used to call "what the heck" syndrome, or you could build yourself up by picking yourself up, dusting yourself off and starting all over again. Fresh start, clean slate. Okay, so you made a mistake. That is why there are erasers on pencils.

What's done is done, the real power is in your next step. You cannot beat yourself up and build yourself up at the same time. You cannot be a victim and victorious at the same time. You cannot feel defeated and empowered at the same time. You cannot slump over and stand tall at the same time. You cannot frown and smile at the same time.

You choose. When I smile, I automatically feel better. Smile. When I stand tall, I feel empowered. Here I stand in my power.

Surround yourself with support, take small steps and always move towards what you want.

***

Part II: You Always Have Time for What You Put First

> *"Focus on the critical few...not the insignificant many." - Author Unknown*

***

When I was a Weight Watchers leader, some of my members used to complain that they did not have enough time in the day to get done all they wanted to do. Whenever I heard this, I always asked, "How many hours do you spend watching TV at night?"

Now, I am not against watching TV. I am against claiming there is no time. Everything in life is about priorities.

Here is a riddle from world renowned success coach, author and motivational speaker, John DiLemme:

I am your constant companion.

I will push you forward to success or I will drag you down in failure.

I am completely at your command.

80% of what you do, you might as well hand over to me and I will do it promptly and I will do it correctly.

I am easily managed; you must merely be firm with me.

Show me what you'd like to have done, and after a couple of lessons, I will do it automatically.

I am the servant of all great people.

Alas, I am the servant of all failures as well.

All who are great, I have made great.

All who are failures, I have made failures.

I am not a machine, but I do work with the precision of a machine and the intellect of a human.

*Take me, train me, be firm with me, and I'll lay the
world at your feet.*

Be easy with me, and I will destroy you!

WHO AM I?

Think about it for a few minutes before continuing.

Have you figured it out?

The answer is habit. The most important habit I practice in my life is prioritizing. I ask myself, "What is most important?" Then I write "To-Do" lists starting with the words, "In The Order Of" to remind myself that we always have time for what we put first.

As a Weight Watchers leader, I put acknowledgement and appreciation first by starting my meetings with celebrations!!! What behavior or milestone are you celebrating? After the celebrations, I would ask, "Why do I start with celebration?"

People would answer, "Because it is positive, it is uplifting, it is FUN."

I would respond, "Yes, those are the reasons I DO celebrations, but the reason I START with celebrations is because 'We always have time for what we put first.'"

Yes, I was trying to drive home the point, so it absolutely delighted me when some of my groups started to answer my question in unison, shouting, "We always have time for what we put first."

Think about it. Don't you always get the first thing on the list done? Life is busy. We don't always have time for everything. But don't you always have time for what you put first?

When Kelly and Michael were very small, probably no older than twelve months, I was sitting on the floor with them, thinking, "This is the happiest time of my life. These two children bring me so much joy and love. This time is probably going to go very fast. I am going to enjoy it." Simple as that. I used to joke to friends that I didn't know where the vacuum was for three years. The truth is that it just wasn't as important as time with Kelly and Michael or sleep. You always have time for what you put first, and they came first. There are only so many seconds in the day, so you must choose wisely.

***

Part III: What Do You Want? Is It Worth It?

"Wanting something is not enough. You must hunger for it. Your motivation must be absolutely compelling in order to overcome the obstacles that will invariably come your way." - Les Brown

***

I liked to do an exercise at my workshops that I called, "What Do You Want?"

The instructions were:

- Find a partner, preferably someone you do not know.
- Decide who is A and who is B.
- Partner A ask Partner B, "What do you want?"
- Partner B answers.
- Again, Partner A asks, "What do you want?"
- Partner B answers another thing they want.
- Repeat until Partner B runs out of things they want, or three minutes are up, whichever comes first.
- Switch and repeat.

Whenever I did this exercise, I would mill around the room, noticing that some people were answering quickly while others seemed to struggle once they named three or four things they wanted. After six minutes, I invited the group to gather back together and share their thoughts about the exercise. The responses were always interesting. Most people had difficulty with the exercise. Some said that as it went on they seemed to go deeper and answered things they didn't even realize they wanted. Others said it seemed so foreign to think about what they wanted that they were almost numb to it. It was difficult to answer again and again what you want. They were waiting for me to stop the

97

exercise, but also surprised that they were struggling to answer. They said that they hadn't given it much thought or intention, like they were living by default instead of by design. The purpose of this exercise is to force you to acknowledge the things that you want and to live with intentionality.

The first two teaching points, "You Can't Be In Two Places At The Same Time" and "You Always Have Time For What You Put First," lead to my third teaching point:

What do you want? Is it worth it?

There are many things we want, but what are we willing to do to get them? Is it worth the time? Is it worth the money? Is it worth the energy? Is it worth the devotion? Is it worth the discipline and sacrifice?

When I give myself permission to really honor what I need and think about what I want, I have clarity and I make decisions for my highest good. I stand in my power and truth.

When I knew I wanted to have children, it was worth receiving multiple insulin injections daily to gain the tightest control of my diabetes.

When I wanted to buy a house, it was worth following a budget, cutting up credit cards, and limiting going out to restaurants.

When I was a leader at Weight Watchers. I would hold up my left hand and ask, "What do you want?" Then I would hold up my right hand and ask, "Is it worth it?"

If you want to see weight loss on the scale, it is worth skipping dessert or taking a walk. If you really want pizza, it is worth taking a longer walk or eating salad for lunch.

When I really know what I want, it becomes worth doing what it takes.

When I wanted to keep my children in private school so they would be challenged more and better prepared for college (not to mention the beautiful courtyard gardens teeming with gorgeous birds--seriously, they had peacocks in the courtyard), it was worth it to take a job as a supermarket manager at Stop & Shop with a consistent salary, even if it meant sacrificing the job I loved as a Weight Watchers leader. I still kept one meeting every week because you cannot deny yourself your passion.

***

As a coach, I found myself repeatedly using the following three teaching points:

You Can't Be in Two Places at the Same Time - You must choose. You can slouch over or stand tall. You can beat yourself up or build yourself up. You can be a victim, or you can be victorious. You can accentuate the negative or you can accentuate the positive. The choice is yours.

You Always Have Time for What You Put First - Make a habit of prioritizing. You do not have time for everything, but the first thing on the list always gets done.

What Do You Want? Is It Worth It? - When you get clear on what you truly want, it makes it easier to determine if it is worth the time, money, effort, devotion, discipline and sacrifice. Honor what you want and determine if it is worth it, and you will move mountains.

Chapter 8: Who Holds The Key?

"If there is no enemy within, the enemy without can do us no harm." - African Proverb

***

My favorite Success Principle is #1: Take 100% Responsibility For Your Life.

No blaming, no complaining. We are 100% responsible for everything in our life. Jack Canfield began a workshop I attended in 2011 by saying, "You remember Martin Luther King's speech, 'I Have A Complaint?'"

Jack made the point that Martin Luther King had plenty of things to complain about and plenty of people to blame, but instead his speech was called, "I Have A Dream." His words made a great impression on me by highlighting that it doesn't really matter what is happening; it is all about how I am going to respond. This principle aligned well with something I used to teach as a Weight Watchers leader: that it doesn't matter what you have already done, what is most important is what your next step will be.

Jack further illustrated his point using the formula, E+R=O. Event + Response = Outcome. Response is our point of power; response is the only thing we truly control and how we respond will determine the outcome of any given situation. After I left that workshop, I began asking myself and my clients, "Who holds the key?" The answer, of course, is that you do. We hold the key to our success, we hold the key to our results, we hold the key to our relationships. It is up to us what we are going to do. Our response equals our results. Our response is what we control. If we are not happy with our results, it is up to us to change our response. We hold the key to our success. If we want to lose weight, then we need to take the actions to lose weight. We need to eat less and move more. Then our results will be different. You are the one in the driver's seat. You hold the key to your results and to your success. A client of mine used to say, "if it is going to be, it is up to me." You hold the key.

***

The same year I attended Jack's workshop, my children Kelly and Michael were graduating from college. I was very proud that my ex-husband and I had co-parented so well since our separation and divorce in 2002. We both chose to put the children first when making decisions. About a month or two before graduation, however, my ex-husband and I had a disagreement about how much his final child support payment should be. I was enraged. I stewed over the situation, thinking, "I can't believe this! We have done so well and now he is going to ruin graduation!"

I was ranting and raving and getting myself all worked up. I was annoyed for a couple of days, complaining and blaming him. After all we had accomplished, now he was going to ruin graduation.

Then I remembered the formula: Event + Response = Outcome.

Our disagreement + my ranting and raving and unwillingness to be around my ex-husband = graduation ruined.

Our disagreement + my cordial behavior and willingness to be around him = a fabulous graduation celebration.

My point of power was my response. My response in all situations was truly all I could control. I stopped at a rest stop on the drive up to Boston for the graduation, looked up to the sky and thanked God for the strength to do what was best for the outcome I wanted. I also silently thanked Jack for the wisdom and knowledge to determine how to do so.

All in all, the graduation was a wonderful celebration and we all had a great time.

Who holds the key? I do.

***

In 2012, I received my Certificate of Completion for Train the Trainer with Jack Canfield to teach the Success Principles. Train the Trainer was a year-long intensive professional training program focused on how to experientially teach the principles of success and the facilitation of individual and group transformation. Shortly after that, an online version was created and anyone who previously graduated and sent a video of their progress was gifted the online version. After I completed the online version, I was invited for a 7-day Certification Week, during I would be given a Success Principle to teach on stage and receive feedback from Jack. I was so excited. I registered and awaited my assigned Success Principle. The Success Principle I was assigned was #3: Decide What You Want, another one of my favorites. I was beyond thrilled to get this one. Once we decide what we want, it is always easier to take action.

As a Weight Watchers leader, I used to hold up my right hand and say, "What do you want?"

Then I would hold up my left hand and say, "Is it worth it?"

This applied to outcomes and food.

I began preparing my presentation. I felt very confident because it was something I taught often, and I was going to do a guided visualization along with music, something I had also done frequently. Of course, I'd be doing the presentation from Jack's stage so that stretched my comfort zone. There was an audience of maybe 80-100. I walked confidently onto the stage. I had been doing public speaking now for over fifteen years. I attended and spoke at Toastmasters as well as Business Network International, so I was very comfortable with public speaking. But it was Jack's stage. I was feeling something akin to exhilaration as I walked onto the stage to speak about Success Principle #3: Decide What You Want. About halfway through the presentation, I motioned to the back of the room to dim the lights and start the music.

The sound guy queued up "Bamboo Flute and Synthesizer" by Jonathan Foust as I led the group through a visualization in which they envisioned what they wanted to accomplish in the next five years. After the visualization, I instructed them in a quick exercise in which they shared with a partner about the experience of the visualization before wrapping up my presentation.

As soon as I finished my presentation, Jack stood up and walked towards the stage to deliver his feedback to me immediately and publicly. I felt the presentation went well but I eagerly awaited Jack's feedback, feeling a mixture of anticipation and excitement. He made eye contact with me as he began saying, "Patty [President of the Canfield Group] and I looked at each other during your presentation and said, 'Noreen has been a part of the Canfield community for some time now, how is this the first time we are seeing her present?'" Jack flashed a smile and I just knew that his feedback would be positive. He continued, "You have great stage presence, good voice projection, you knew your material and presented it well. You could slow down a little." I'm a New Yorker, what do you expect? But he had a good point. "You did a good job with the visualization, I really liked your choice of music. I suggest you find other words to say than 'I want you to.' I will send you a book recommendation along with the written notes from my feedback. Overall, you did a great job!"

I was extremely thrilled. I walked off the stage floating on cloud nine, feeling proud for having the confidence to believe in myself and present on Jack's stage, but the real test was still to come...

Throughout the week, Jack had been inviting people to come to the stage and lead a meditation or lead an energizer. I wanted to lead a yoga dance to "Like It Or Not," by Madonna, as an energizer. The lyrics to the chorus always energized me: "This is who I am, like it or not. You can love me or leave me, I am never going to stop." I even had movements that went with it. I was so excited, so at the end of one of the days I went up to Jack and asked if I could do an energizer to the song. He told me to write it on an index card so he would remember it

(Success Principle #3: Decide What You Want and Success Principle #17: Ask, Ask, Ask.) I was flying high.

When I arrived in the room the next day, I ran up to the sound guy in the back, showed him my iPod and said, "If Jack calls me up, this is the song I want you to play."

I was really thinking "when" Jack calls me up, but the day passed by and Jack never called me up. At the end of the day, I wrote my request again, but instead of using a white index card like the day before, I used a pink index card so it would stand out. When I handed it to him, he laughed, gestured to the other one on his stand and then said, "Okay, give me that one, maybe I will see it better." Success Principle #22: Practice Persistence.

The next day came and went and he still didn't call me up, but that didn't deter me.

The next day I entered the room wearing a bright pink shirt with a giant dancing Om sign on the front and sat in the front row. Surely, he'd have to call me up. The day came and went, and he still didn't call on me.

Now, we have arrived at the last day. As I arrived for the morning session, I read the words, "Questions and Comments," up on the screen. I knew the afternoon was going to be graduation, so I sat down and began to feel a bit disappointed. I really thought Jack was going to let me lead that dance. I was just about to complain and blame him when I thought, "Don't blame Jack. You can either get on the plane feeling all disappointed or you can raise your hand and tell Jack you really wanted to lead the dance." My heart pounded really hard as I got up the nerve to say something (Success Principle #15: Experience the Fear and Take Action Anyway). When the previous participant finished her question, I felt my hand dart up as my heart pounded and my throat grew dry! The assistant handed me the mic and I said, "You know, Jack, I really wanted to lead a dance!"

Jack flashed a smile and said, "Noreen, do you want to lead a dance?"

I almost exploded, "YES!!!"

He responded, "Well, do you have the music?"

I immediately pulled my iPod out of my pocket, already queued up to the right song, and shouted, "YES!"

Jack said, "Okay, I will take one more question while Noreen sets up the music." At this point, I was ecstatic as I ran back to the sound table to give Bob the sound guy my iPod to play the song. Jack finished answering the last question and then invited everyone to the big open area in the back of the room where there is space to move. Someone gave me a mic and I asked Trish, one of the assistants, to help me in the demo. Before the song starts playing, I walked Jack through a quick rehearsal, saying the words to the chorus and doing the choreography, then having Jack repeat them as I demonstrate the movements. After going through it three or four times, I instructed the group that before the chorus of the song, we will move through the room giving each other high fives and saying, "HA!," to clear the stale air out of the lungs. Finally, I look over at Bob and say, "Hit it."

The music started playing and the group, including Jack and the assistants, began moving through the room, high fiving and saying, "HA!" When the chorus started, I told everyone to find a partner to do the choreographed movements and then go back to the high fives and the Ha!

What a blast!!! Jack danced with us, everyone had fun and one of the assistants had recorded it for me. It was so worth putting my hand up, with my heart pounding, and taking 100% responsibility. Who held the key? I did.

When I went up on stage later that day to receive my certificate, Jack smiled and gave me a big high five and said, "HA!"

What a memorable experience.

In the end, it comes right back to Success Principle #1: Take 100% Responsibility For Your Life.

No blaming, no complaining. Event + Response = Outcome.

Our response is always our point of power. Here I stand in my power. You do not always control the events, but you do always control your response and therefore, control the outcome.

I did not give up and I did not wait for Jack. I raised my hand and that changed everything. It was so fun, so empowering and so memorable!

Who holds the key? I do.

At my workshops and retreats, I put keys on a ribbon and distribute to the attendees or hand out as a prize to remind them that they hold the key.

Who holds the key? You do!

Chapter 9: Mirror, Mirror on the Wall, Who Do You Acknowledge Most of All?

"This above all: to thine own self be true." - William Shakespeare

***

On the sunny morning of August 13, 2011, I took a cab to the airport to fly to Phoenix, Arizona to attend Jack Canfield's Breakthrough to Success Training. Little did I know then what a breakthrough it was going to be. I felt good because I was traveling on the 13th and 13 has always been my lucky number. After landing in Phoenix, I boarded a Super Shuttle, where I immediately met three women who were also attending BTS-Alice, Theresa, and Christine. Theresa would eventually become my accountability partner and somebody with whom I've shared five commitments on a daily basis ever since. As we drove to the hotel, I felt full of joyful expectations. For the previous three years I had wanted to attend this event. I had come with the intention of developing a business plan, but what I received was so much deeper than that. As we entered the room on the first day, a group of assistants greeted us as they danced to the upbeat music playing from the speakers, which encouraged all of us to dance all the way to our seats. What a fabulous way to start the day. We also had the option to participate in a yoga class each morning before breakfast, which even had gluten-free muffins! I thought I had died and gone to heaven. Music filled each day as we practiced meditation, self-awareness exercises and experiential learning. Jack is very skilled at getting groups to bond early in the training. He taught us the benefit and proper technique for giving a silent hug. Even after only the first few days, I felt I had already learned so much.

Towards the end of the week, I asked Theresa, who lived in Nashville, Tennessee, if she would like to be my accountability partner. Living in New York, I was not sure how it would work, but I was open to the possibilities. We began the following week with our daily phone calls by using Success Principle #23: Practice the Rule of Five. Each day, we would tell each other our five intentions for the day and report on how we did with the previous day's intentions. For two weeks, Theresa listed the "mirror exercise," one of the exercises Jack taught us at BTS. After hearing her day after day, I finally said, "I don't really need the mirror exercise, I have always had high self-esteem and self-confidence."

She replied, "Oh, that's not what the mirror exercise is about. It is about ACKNOWLEDGING yourself." I envisioned the word "ACKNOWLEDGING" in flashing lights on Broadway. I stood frozen in one spot in my kitchen and thought about my yoga teacher, Janice. Sometimes, as I was leaving her class, she would acknowledge something I had overcome in my life and she would say, "Really, you are amazing." I would walk to the car standing a little taller, recalling the event and her statement and think, "Wow, that was amazing!" This was my "A-HA" moment. Maybe Theresa was on to something…

I thought about how I believed acknowledgement and appreciation is so important to success. For the employees I managed, the clients I coached, the students to whom I taught yoga, and most importantly, for my children, Kelly and Michael. And yet, I so rarely acknowledged and appreciated myself. I immediately added the mirror exercise to my list and looked forward to getting to 40 consecutive days as Jack had instructed. If I missed one day, I had to start over!

The first few days felt uncomfortable because I had to look into the mirror and use my name:

"Noreen, I acknowledge you for packing those five boxes."

"Noreen, I am so proud of you for taking a walk this morning when you really did not want to get up."

"Noreen, I am so proud of you for eating an apple instead of the chocolate."

"Noreen, I love you!!"

Those first few days I looked into the mirror, saying, "Wow, you really have very blue eyes. You have blue eyes like Grandpa." I would do a few days, but then I would forget and would have to begin again. Finally, I realized that if I did not miss a day, then Christmas Eve would be day #40. I decided this would be my Christmas gift to myself. I put sticky notes on my alarm clock and the mirror in the bathroom where I brushed my teeth. On Christmas Eve, I celebrated 40 days! I began to truly develop such an intimate relationship with myself and looked forward to my evening ritual so much that I decided to keep going and see if I could do it for 365 days. When I put my mind to something, I tend to take it to the next level. I've been told I can be a bit intense.

I also began sharing the exercise with my clients, most of whom were very uncomfortable at first, just as I had been. Some tried to make it a bit humorous, some were very willing, some were brought to tears, and some were simply not willing to do it. Their reactions made me realize how powerful this exercise was. For me and for some of my clients, the exercise went hand in hand with another one of Jack's exercises in which you say, "MY needs are just as important as your needs," and the other person says, "Yes, they are, Noreen." Then your partner says, "MY needs are just as important as your needs," and I would say, "Yes, they are, Theresa."

As I worked towards my 365 Days, I found myself always being mindful of all the positive things I was doing. Not only was I more aware of these things, but I was also looking at myself in the mirror and deeply connecting with myself. It felt like a daily ritual of blessing and honoring myself. I moved into using what I call the "Power of the Pause"--stopping before I made a decision or answered a request and saying to myself, "My needs are just as important as your needs." This always resulted in a better decision. No anger. No resentment. No guilt. I incorporated these lessons and strategies in my coaching practice and I was seeing better results. After I celebrated Day #365, I thought, "Why would I ever stop?"

Imagine when you first fell in love or when your child or grandchild was born, looking deeply into their eyes with love, admiration, and respect. The vibration is so high, and you are feeling amazing. There is nothing you would not do for this person, nothing you would not do for their highest good, their health and well-being. Now imagine this person is YOU. I have always considered myself a strong, self-confident person, but after passing 2,500 days of practicing the mirror exercise (I told you I could be a bit intense!), along with incorporating many other Success Principles, I continue to attract wonderful things into my life daily. I am moving through a list of 101 goals I made at the 2011 BTS almost effortlessly. The MAGIC is in the action. The most important thing I have incorporated into my life is the mirror exercise, or shall we call it the Miracle Exercise? When we connect intimately with ourselves, we honor and bless ourselves, we notice and nurture, and we live a more purposeful life with fewer attachments. When we look inside, we see that we have everything we need. We just never looked deep enough or long enough. When you fully love and honor yourself, you are able to fully love and honor everyone else.

In 2013, I changed the name of the mirror exercise to The Compassionate Mirror Ritual. It had become a wonderful daily evening ritual of acknowledgement and compassion.

Around that time Jack emailed me and asked what I felt was the biggest benefit of doing the mirror exercise daily for so many days. Without hesitation, I immediately emailed him and said there are many benefits but the biggest benefit for me was developing an intimate relationship with myself. After all, I am the only person I will spend my entire life with. Jack responded by asking if he could have permission to share the story on his Facebook page. I was honored, and of course, I said, "Yes!"

The next time I saw him in person, I said, "Thanks for posting my story on your Facebook page."

He replied, "It is a great story. Thank YOU!" To this day, he still emails me every so often just to ask how many days I'm up to.

I have shared The Compassionate Mirror Ritual at Let Your Yoga Dance Teacher Training in Massachusetts, at retreats with Karen Drucker in Monterrey, California, at my weekend retreats in New York, and at a five-day retreat in Jamaica. Now, I can say that the ritual is not only coast-to-coast but also international. And of course, it is, because the ritual is such a powerful practice. I love to share it with others and support them in beginning their practice, one small glorious step at a time. When I started my 40 days, I had no idea it would blossom into a more than seven-year ritual. Yahoo!

Initially, I was mostly drawn to continue because I was creating a deep connection with myself. Looking into my eyes every evening to acknowledge and love myself became this wonderful practice of intimacy. I felt like I was getting to know myself better and sharing more freely and honestly.

The practice moved into strengthening my self-acknowledgement and love muscle. It became natural to acknowledge and appreciate ME. I moved into an atmosphere of constant awareness as I always looked for positive things throughout the day to acknowledge that night in the mirror. When there was something really good to acknowledge, I would rush to find a mirror so I could acknowledge it with the enthusiasm that I was feeling in the moment.

After 5 ½ years of practicing my wonderful Compassionate Mirror Ritual, I was diagnosed with Multiple Sclerosis. That was when I fully realized the accumulative benefits of this practice. After the diagnosis at the hospital, my family went home, and I went into the bathroom. First, I sobbed in disbelief for what seemed like twenty minutes but was probably more like five minutes. Then, I looked deeply into my eyes and thought, "Now, you really need compassion. What can you do for your highest good? How do you want to show up for all of this?" I thought of my favorite Success Principle #1: Take 100% Responsibility For Your Life.

Event + Response = Outcome. Response is our point of power.

I looked into the mirror that night and said:

"Noreen, I acknowledge you for feeling your feelings and allowing yourself to sob."

"Noreen, I am so proud of you for asking the question, how do I want to show up for this?"

"Noreen, I acknowledge you for doing the Compassionate Mirror Ritual tonight."

"Noreen, I love you."

"Noreen, you deserve the very best!"

***

Now, I think it is time to do a TED Talk about the Compassionate Mirror Ritual. On November 15, 2018, I celebrated seven consecutive years without missing a day, that's 2,555 days and counting! There are many phases, stages and benefits to the Compassionate Mirror Ritual. It is a practice. When I began with the 40-Day challenge, I did not ever think I would be doing it for seven years and counting!

Self-love is a powerful practice. Practice, because just like the piano, if we want to become proficient, we must practice. My advice to you is to just start. Small steps lead to big success.

Chapter 10: I Am So Blessed

"A blessing is a circle of light drawn around a person to protect, heal and strengthen." - John O'Donohue

***

When I was pregnant with my twins and started to feel the fluttering in my belly and felt something come to life, I realized I wanted to come to life too. Something magnificent was occurring inside me and I wanted to feel every precious moment. If I wanted to feel the joy, I could no longer push down the pain. That fluttering of life arrived as a blessing. The biggest blessing of my life. The birth of my children invited me to look at the world through a different lens, one in which I was willing to feel the pain, feel the joy, and allow past wounds to begin to heal.

In September 2013, I attended Let Your Yoga Dance Teacher Training, where I first heard the song, "I Am So Blessed," by Karen Drucker. Let Your Yoga Dance is an activity in which the principles of yoga practice are combined with the sheer joy of dancing to bring more mindfulness and healing to the body, heart, mind and soul. While teaching us about dance prayers, program director Megha Nancy Buttenheim played this song because dance prayer is all about connecting with one's inner wisdom and the song moves at a soothing pace that allows the listener to connect more deeply with herself. The world outside my body faded away as I listened to the lyrics:

I am so blessed,

I am so blessed,

I am so grateful for all that I have.

I am so blessed,

I am so blessed,

I am so grateful,

I am so blessed.

I really felt like the song was about my life. I had been through so much and received so many blessings. I felt called to express my gratitude for those blessings and acknowledge the people in my life whom I consider blessings, those who have helped me heal, protected me and strengthened me.

When I began to teach my own Let Your Yoga Dance (LYYD) classes, I put together different playlists and choreographed different dances for each class, but "I Am So Blessed" remained constant on the playlist even as all the other songs changed. After using the song in my private coaching, at workshops, retreats, and LYYD classes for over two years, I felt inspired one day to reach out to Karen Drucker directly to request permission to include her music on the website for my business. She replied to my message to give me permission and could not have been nicer. We began emailing back and forth and discovered that we had many mutual acquaintants such as Jack Canfield, Tama Kieves, and Jana Stanfield. After striking up an online friendship, I attended a retreat she was facilitating in Monterey, California in June 2016. Meeting in person, we felt an instant connection, like we had been friends for years. What a fabulous time!

A few months later, I assisted Karen at a retreat she was facilitating on the East Coast at Kripalu in the Berkshires. I felt honored, privileged, and blessed to lead the class in a dance on August 27, what would have been my father's 97th birthday, while Karen sang, "I Am So Blessed." My eyes filled with tears as I dedicated the song to my father, Francis Michael Kelty. I felt so blessed and so grateful to have had him as a dad. The healing had truly come full circle.

***

In September 2001, I began attending yoga classes at New York Sports Club led by a kind, gentle woman named Janice. A skilled teacher with a big heart, her essence of kindness immediately resonated with me. To set the theme for each class, Janice would begin with a reading from *A Grateful Heart: Daily Blessings for the Evening Meal from Buddha to the Beatles*. She would also end with a reading, usually connecting back to the original theme. Her class was so much more than just going through the postures. She also focused on teaching the principles of yoga philosophy, referring to yoga off the mat as well as yoga on the mat.

In addition to teaching yoga, Janice worked full-time as a professional therapist. After a few months of attending her yoga class and developing a trusting relationship with her, I scheduled an appointment with her to begin counseling to help me navigate my way through my divorce.

As I pulled in the tree-lined driveway to Our Lady of Grace Retreat Center for my first session, I felt a sense of serenity amidst the beauty of the trees and the lush green grass. I entered a small house off to the right of the parking lot and found myself in a beautifully decorated room that felt like it could be somebody's living room. As soon as I settled in to one of the big, comfortable armchairs, I felt so cozy and immediately knew I made the right decision. Janice had created a very safe space for me. I trusted her. Throughout the course of our conversation, I felt seen and understood. Janice created a safe cocoon to share and heal.

Over the past seventeen years, Janice has been a constant in my life, offering protection and support to me during my divorce, multiple job changes, my mother's death, my children going off to college, selling my house after 26 years and the challenges that have come since being diagnosed with Multiple Sclerosis. Everyone should be so blessed to have someone like Janice in their life. I am grateful for her presence and all the things she has taught me.

When I was beating myself up over having feelings for somebody who was already in a relationship (nothing happened, mind you), Janice asked me "SO WHAT?!" clearly demonstrating to me the importance of practicing self-compassion without judgment.

She also taught me that "there is room for it all," good feelings, bad feelings, positive experiences, negative experiences. All of it can happen at the same time.

Practicing self-compassion without judgment and allowing room for it all have helped to protect, heal, and strengthen. I am so blessed. I am so grateful.

***

The biggest blessing of my life has been my two wonderful children, Kelly and Michael. From the very beginning, Kelly was my little angel. One night when she was a few months old, I sat in a rocking chair in my house with Kelly's head snuggled tightly against my chest. I held my hand to her back, feeling her precious heartbeat and the warmth of her body. The house was so quiet that I could listen to her soft breaths while she slept. I felt so content. All was right in the world. What an intense, wonderful feeling.

Kelly has always been so thoughtful and so caring. She provided strength by assisting me at some of my earliest workshops as well as my five-day retreat in Jamaica and attending my weekly Let Your Yoga Dance classes with her boyfriend, Chris, while also promoting the classes to others. As a little girl, she loved to make drawings of flowers and sun and write, "To Mommy, Love Kelly." Whenever I look at those drawings, I feel so blessed for the sunshine she has brought into my life.

When Kelly and Michael were infants, I nursed them separately overnight. One night, I picked Michael up to walk from the nursery to the den. As I carried him, I noticed he had the biggest, brightest smile on his face. His beaming smile was infectious, and I couldn't help but feel the joy. When he was five years old, he got off the bus with the same beaming smile. They had a Christmas shopping fair at school that day and I overheard him tell Kelly that he got me a diamond ring. He made me close my eyes and open my hands. When I opened my eyes, I saw the ring in my hands, but it was the expression on his face that was absolutely priceless. I felt blessed to have this little boy who was so excited to give me a gift he had picked out himself.

I saw that same beaming smile on the day of Michael's wedding when he played guitar and sang "Green Eyes" to his new bride, Sarah. As he sang, I began to feel my father's presence in the room. My father had been a singer and I like to think that Michael's voice grew stronger as he went on because of my father's presence, which I have never felt more strongly than I did that day. I felt blessed that Michael helped to bridge the generations and allow my healing to continue.

I have often said (and been made fun of by family members for saying, "I have the best kids!" After twenty-nine years as a mother, that remains the truth. Kelly and Michael have taught me so much about life and love. Shortly after they were born, I wrote "The Happiest Days of My Life" (and they were!) on the cover of a black marble notebook in which I would write stories about their childhood and occasionally glue photos on the front and back cover. Although it was not always easy to find the time, I am glad I did so back then. It brings a smile to my face to revisit some of those precious moments and delight in some of the stories I wrote but did not remember.

I have many blessings in my life, but Kelly and Michael are at the top of the list. They continue to protect, heal and strengthen me.

I am so blessed. I am so grateful.

Chapter 11: I Feel Good!

"Peace begins when expectation ends." - Sri Chinnoy

***

When I was a little girl, I asked my mother what she wanted for Christmas one year. She responded, "All I want is peace and quiet." Easier said than done with a husband and four daughters to take care of, not to mention our dog, Precious.

As an adult, I've often felt the same way, seeking the gift of peace. I've found that in stillness, the answers come.

When I let go of expectations, I feel good.

Especially the expectations I have of others. How they should act, how they should respond. When I release my expectations of myself and others, I find peace.

***

Shortly after I began working for Weight Watchers, I began recruiting staff members by visiting various centers in Nassau County, Queens, Brooklyn, Staten Island, the Bronx, and Westchester. One day, I was visiting a center at the Cross-County Shopping Center in Yonkers and one of the members said, "I feel good." I responded by singing the chorus to "I Feel Good" by James Brown. The members laughed and one of them told me that there was a store in the mall that sold a James Brown doll that sang the song. Of course, I had to have it.

I started to incorporate the doll into my regular meetings. Whenever somebody said the words, "I feel good," I pressed the button and danced around a little. People loved it. Isn't that what we all want, to feel good? Once you feel good, you will make better decisions.

Almost a decade later, I was waiting to be seated for breakfast at a restaurant in Montauk, which is about 100 miles east of Nassau County on the very end of Long Island. Suddenly, I heard someone singing "I FEEL GOOD." I turned and saw one of my former members, Marianne, sitting on the bench smiling.

Another time I was walking on the first level at Roosevelt Field Mall when I heard a voice from the second level singing "I FEEL GOOD." I looked up and spotted another former member, Helene, hanging over the rail waving. Obviously, the message stuck with people. Singing the song helped make losing weight fun.

Singing the song also reminded me to notice when I'm feeling good and acknowledge the feeling. Appreciate it. Over the years, I've noticed that I always FEEL GOOD when I let go of expectations. But, of course, that doesn't mean that I never have expectations.

When I held a retreat in Jamaica, I expected sunshine and warm weather. I expected to dance on the beach. I expected to fill all eighteen spots available for registration. None of which happened.

Ten people registered for the retreat. I could have been disappointed that I didn't max out the registration, or I could release my expectations and focus on the critical few who decided to register. Because the classes would be smaller, my impact on each individual could be larger and create stronger connections between the attendees.

On the first full day of the retreat, the skies opened, and rain poured down all day. So long, sunshine! I could have despaired about not being able to dance on the beach, or I could create a dance party on our covered platform, protected from the elements while still enjoying nature all around us.

I began each morning by meditating as the sun rose. On the second morning, I had an epiphany as the line came back to me, "Peace begins when expectation ends." That morning during yoga, I instructed everyone to lie down on their mats for the start of the class. After some relaxing breathing, I told the class, "Peace begins when expectation ends. Not just here in Jamaica, but in our lives. Release all your retreat expectations and open yourself up to all the hidden treasures. If we just release our expectations, sometimes even greater treasures than we could have imagined will reveal themselves to us."

After that session, the group settled in to share the adventure, ready to experience the hidden treasures. As part of a ritual I had planned for later in the retreat in which participants wrote down something that they wanted to release on a piece of paper and threw it into a fire we had built, I wrote only one word, "Expectation."

On the last day of the retreat, after all activities had been completed, I walked down to the platform by myself, put some calming music on, set up cushions under my chest to open my heart posture, rolled a blanket under my neck and laid down on my yoga mat. I invited a breath deep down. On the exhale, I felt a tear run down the side of my face. I closed my eyes and continued breathing. The outside world melted away as I drifted inside myself. The retreat was over. A very successful and fun experience for everyone. I had received excellent feedback and now it was time to relax. The tears continued to trickle down my cheeks as I released the emotions I hadn't allowed myself to feel, emotions tied to the expectations I had set for my life, expectations that weighed heavily on my soul. I had been divorced for fifteen years but hadn't yet released the expectations I had for my marriage. When I got married, I expected it to be happily ever after, I expected to grow old together, I expected to have a lifelong partner. Awareness is all part of the healing. I continued to lie on my back, quietly listening to the sounds of the birds and animals and feeling the breeze against my cheeks. When I was finished, I gathered my things walked back to my room, feeling lighter. I thought, "I am leaving these expectations in Jamaica." Then I laughed, thinking, "You had to come all the way to Jamaica to release these expectations?"

I felt good.

***

A few months after the retreat in Jamaica, I registered for a retreat that Karen Drucker was holding in Monterey, California. I felt so excited, but I truly had no expectations. I remained open to unlimited possibilities. I just wanted to meet Karen. Then Karen emails me and asks, "Would you like to lead a dance to one of my songs? We can work it out when you get here."

Do fish swim? Do dogs bark? I was waiting for someone to come out and say, "You are on Candid Camera!" Of course, I would love to lead a dance with Karen singing. I was thrilled. In disbelief but thrilled. So, I packed my multi-colored LED lights with rubber bands to place on fingers for dancing and booked a flight. On the flight to California, I read a book that Karen had written called, "Let Go of the Shore," in which she writes, "This is my path. It is a constant process of surrendering to what is, what is next, who I am, what is emerging, what needs to be released. It's about letting go of the safety of the shore and what I have known, while floating into the mystery that is this amazing life."

I loved her more after reading it. I arrived with just enough time to drop off my bag, freshen up and get to the location for a little pre-dinner meetup. I squealed when I saw Karen, prompting a few women who were standing nearby to laugh but I didn't care. I ran up to her and started hugging her. Then I said, "You know who I am, right???"

She laughed and said "Yes, Noreen, I know who you are." The weekend was off to an amazing start. No expectations. I FELT GOOD.

I led yoga on the beach Friday and Saturday with the Pacific Ocean behind me. It was an extraordinary experience. Karen kept asking me to get up and make up dances. Everything felt so effortless. On Saturday night, Karen held a segment called Expressing Yourself, in which people read a poem, sing a song, or do some kind of demonstration. When Karen called my name, I walked up to the front of the room, kicked off my shoes, asked everyone to move back their chairs and handed a box of finger lights to each side of the room to pass out. I wish I had a photo of the expression on Karen's face as she said, "Oh, maybe we should wait for last for you!" So, I sat back down and patiently waited until all the other participants had gone. Then I finished passing out the finger lights and instructed the group on the choreography for "Gifts of the Goddess." Just telling this story is filling my body with JOY!

Karen began playing the music and singing as I led the movements. The colorful lights looked gorgeous in the night darkness as the women moved their hands with the music. When we finished, Karen said, "THAT WAS FABULOUS! Do you want to do another?"

So, then we did "Thank You For this Day," after which she raised her right arm out to me and said, "MY NEW DANCE CAPTAIN." I was beyond BLISS. The entire weekend Thursday through Sunday was exceptional. So effortless and flowing. Everything was in sync. I had no expectations and it just flowed. Karen said she saw the joy in my dance and was honored to be part of it. I am forever grateful to Karen for that amazing weekend.

I felt so supported. I felt so good.

Chapter 12: Our Lives Are The Direct Result Of The Stories We Tell

"Change your thoughts, change your world." -
Norman Vincent Peale

***

When I was a little girl, I was responsible, I got good grades in school, and I kept my bedroom neat. My father always appreciated when I helped around the house and my grandparents always made a big deal over me doing well in school. My grandfather always said I was going to run my own business, so the story I began to tell myself was that I am STRONG, SMART and CAPABLE. On the surface, that sounds pretty good, but looking back now, I realize it also created the belief that my needs were not as important as other people's needs. After all, I could take care of myself. At some point, I also began to think I didn't need love.

I looked up to my grandmother, who didn't appear to need love either. At her own husband's funeral, she stood alone in the doorway of the funeral parlor with her head held high, shoulders back, no tears. At the time, I thought this symbolized strength and wisdom, but I realize now that I have no idea what she was feeling.

Much like Nana, I got into the habit of not asking for help. I became the "good little soldier" and toughed it out. After being diagnosed with

Diabetes in November 1972 and my father dying in January 1973, I began to tell myself that I was a survivor who could handle anything.

Being the good little soldier, toughing it out and not asking for help has its consequences. At the end of a very difficult double-risk pregnancy in which I spent the final sixty-three days on total bed rest, I gave birth six weeks early to twins via Cesarean section. As I lay on the operating table being stitched up by the doctor, feeling completely drained emotionally and physically, I probably needed support and love more than at any other time in my life. But because I told myself that I was the good little soldier, I didn't ask for any help. In fact, I encouraged my husband, Mike, to leave my side to go call his mother and share the news because I knew he was excited to tell her and I treated his needs as more important than my needs. After he left the room, I asked the doctor for an additional blanket because I felt so cold that my teeth were chattering. Looking back on this experience, I feel sad that I created a scenario in which I was left alone, cold and trembling, because I told myself that I could handle it.

***

Another familiar story I created as a child was that money causes problems.

I thought that belief came from the fact that my father started to have money problems a few months before he died, which may be partly true but does not tell the whole story.

While attending a workshop called The Rhythm of Money, the instructor asked us to write our earliest bad memory of money. I remembered being eight years old and watching my father, his two brothers and their uncle fight viciously about money and selling my grandmother's house after she died. My mother's father witnessed this as well and told me, "Money changes people, families always fight about money. You need to have clear instructions in your will." The instructor asked other questions like, what money types were your primary caregivers? What were the comments about money from your primary caregivers? What were some of the beliefs and comments around you about money when you were a child?

I began to realize that my beliefs about money were multi-faceted and stemmed from several formative experiences during my childhood. The story I had constructed in my head went something like this. Not only did money cause problems, but you needed to have a job so you could pay the bills. There was no such thing as following your dreams or pursuing your passions. A job was simply a means to end. You worked, you got paid, you paid your bills. Lather, rinse, repeat.

I attempted to change that limiting belief into an empowering belief by saying, "I can make a lot of money doing what I love!!!" I also began telling myself, "Noreen, you deserve the very best" as part of The Compassionate Mirror Ritual.

In March 2015, there was a retreat being held in Jamaica that I really wanted to attend (this is before I held my own retreat in Jamaica, mind you), but I struggled with making the decision to go. I was running my own business and felt reluctant spending the money, since I was making less than I had when I worked for somebody else. Again, I nearly fell into that old story of being the good little soldier and not recognizing that my needs are as important as everyone else's. Once I realized that, I started to pump myself up, telling myself that I DESERVED it.

As I sat on the plane waiting to take off, I said to myself, "I am going to caption this trip: You Deserve The Very Best!" Only moments later, a couple came over to me to say that I was sitting in one of their seats. Apparently, the airline had double-booked my seat. The flight attendant resolved this problem by telling me, "Ms. Kelty, we are going to have to move you up to business/first class."

She carried my yoga mat as I followed her up to business class. As I stretched out in my roomy seat, she offered me coffee served in a real china cup and asked if I would like an omelet with fruit or a frittata for breakfast. I noticed the woman across the aisle drinking champagne, so I asked if I could get a glass of champagne. As she took my order, I thought, "Wow, this is working fast, I got coffee in a china mug, a delicious omelet with a side of fruit, and a glass of champagne!"

When the flight attendant returned and handed me the champagne she asked, "Will there be anything else, Ms. Kelty?"

I thought, "Oh, there will be plenty more," but with a big smile on my face, I answered, "No, thank you very much!"

From that day on, I decided that the story I would tell myself is that "I deserve the very best" and "money flows easily into my life." That is my story and I am sticking to it.

***

The more I explore the more I learn, grow and appreciate. I realize the good little soldier has served me well at times and prepared me for so much. On the other hand, the dancing Jeannie has also served me well. She reminds me to always follow my wildest dreams, play and have fun. Always remember what lights you up. Embrace a higher vibration. There is room for it all. Responsibility and Joy. It is all about balance. Now my story is that I feel fortunate to have a good little soldier and dancing Jeannie in me. Facts are neutral. We give them meaning. In the words of William Shakespeare, "Nothing is either good or bad, it is thinking that makes it so."

Beliefs are ideas we think are true and use as a basis for daily action. They can be empowering, or they can be limiting. They are empowering when they allow us to do things we would not otherwise do. Beliefs are limiting when they stop us from doing things that help us achieve our goals and happiness. Beliefs motivate us and strongly influence our behavior because they live in our hearts as well as our minds. Positive words create the kinds of thoughts that will help make you feel and perform better. What you say is what you get. Our words build our attitude. Words affect our personal power. Our brain hears every word we say. The words that we use are always filtering into our subconscious mind and becoming part of our character. I have always favored choosing words to build myself up rather than beat myself up. That is why years ago I thought the name of my book was going to be "You

Can't Be In Two Places at One Time." Accentuate the positive. I think you can talk yourself into or out of anything. It's all about the story you tell.

Our lives are a direct result of the stories we tell. Our beliefs lead to our stories. Do you have limiting beliefs? Do you have empowering beliefs? Do you believe it is possible? Do you use positive self-talk?

Whatever stories you are telling yourself is creating your life. The good news is that you are the author, director and star of your story. If you do not like what is happening, change your story. Remember most of those stories were made up when we were very young. They stayed in our subconscious and travel along with us as adults unless we become aware, intentional and change the story.

If you don't like the story, change it. It's that simple.

Chapter 13: A Blessing in Disguise

"If we never experience the chill of a dark winter, it is very unlikely that we will ever cherish the warmth of a bright summer's day. Nothing stimulates our appetite for the simple joys of life more than the starvation caused by sadness or desperation. In order to complete our amazing life journey successfully, it is vital that we turn each and every dark tear into a pearl of wisdom, and find the blessing…" - Anthon St. Maarten

***

I woke up on the cool Sunday morning of December 11, 2016, feeling a slight numbness and tingling sensation in my pelvic area, but I didn't think much of it. I gathered up all my supplies for the Living in Joy workshop I was facilitating that day and drove the forty minutes from my apartment to Astoria, Queens to pick up my daughter, Kelly, who was assisting me at the workshop. It was the first time I was at this particular yoga studio, so I was unsure how many attendees would show up. When I checked with the manager the Friday before, only two people were registered. By Saturday, there were four, and by Sunday there were eight. I was happy with eight. Eight people would make for a good workshop.

After I picked up Kelly, we drove to the yoga studio to set up the music and dancing props. As people arrived, they introduced themselves and I asked them to share why they came today. We started with some gratitude partner exercises and I distributed handouts for them to take home for more information and practice exercises for creating a "Living in Joy" lifestyle. We then danced through the chakras (the energy centers of the body) for the next hour and fifteen minutes. We came down onto yoga mats, did a compassionate foot massage with sesame oil while beautiful music played, and finished with a final relaxation, Savasana.

The group was in a great mood. Even the participants who had arrived cranky and said they had nothing to be grateful for said they changed their minds. They felt joy, gratitude and connection from the music and joyful movement. Kelly and I packed up and straightened the room. By the time we got upstairs, the receptionist at the desk said everyone had so much fun and had wonderful things to say on the way out. She encouraged me to contact the owner to schedule another workshop. I left feeling good and thinking that 2016 had been a banner year as far as I was concerned.

Every year since 2009, I had been making Win Lists, lists of your wins or accomplishments over the past year meant to shift your energy and gain momentum towards the next year's goals, in the beginning of December. For 2016, I was already up to six pages and not finished. My list included:

- Receiving a hair, makeup and clothes makeover from Patty Aubery, the president of Jack Canfield's company
- Assisting Jack Canfield at Breakthrough to Success
- Having my story, "Mirror, Mirror on the Wall, Who Do You Acknowledge Most of All?" published in Jack Canfield's Living The Success Principles book,
- Leading an international retreat in Jamaica
- Creating a workbook for my retreats

- Leading yoga on the beach at a retreat with Karen Drucker at Asilomar
- Leading a dance to "Gifts of the Goddess" with Karen singing live that she posted to her YouTube station and shared in her newsletter
- Assisting Karen and Joan Borysenko at Kripalu
- Assisting Megha for Intro to Yoga and Meditation twice at Kripalu
- Leading yoga on the beach in Florida
- Expanding my private coaching business
- Conducting Success Principle and Yoga Dance workshops at new yoga studios
- Assisting Jack Canfield at his seminar, One Day To Greatness

I was feeling like I had accomplished a lot and looked forward to making my goals list for 2017.

When I woke up the Monday after that Living in Joy workshop, I felt tingling in my feet. By Tuesday, the tingling spread to my calves. By Wednesday, I felt the tingling in my thighs and decided to make an appointment with my endocrinologist. On Thursday, I could not feel the pedals in my car and decided not to drive. I asked my former husband, Mike, to drive me to my endocrinologist appointment on Friday.

After examining me and hearing about my symptoms, Dr. Tibaldi recommended I see a neurologist. He tried to get me an appointment but the earliest he could get was Tuesday, December 20. On Saturday, I went with my daughter, Kelly, to see Mariah Carey perform at the Beacon Theater. As I walked up the steps, I noticed that I could not feel my feet on the steps. There was no handrail, so I was grabbing the seats on the right to steady myself until I reached a point at which the seats were filled with people and I had nothing to hold on to. I called to Kelly who was walking ahead of me. When she turned around, she said she saw a man on the left had his arm out to support me. She came running down and grabbed my arm. My heart was pounding, I felt so scared. I could not feel the steps under my feet. I felt total panic. Two scary days followed as I waited for my appointment with the neurologist.

When Tuesday finally arrived, and I went to the neurologist, he immediately told me to go to the emergency room to be admitted. Mike had driven me to the appointment, so he notified Kelly and Michael and then drove me to the hospital, where they began extensive testing. The doctor mentioned it might be Multiple Sclerosis and that if it were MS, he would treat it with five days of steroids, which he began before finishing tests, so that I could still go home for Christmas. Because they weren't sure, I also had blood work done, received x-rays, and underwent a CAT scan. The doctors were not ruling anything out, nor were they confirming their suspicions about MS.

After receiving those tests, a doctor came to my bedside and said I was going to need an MRI that would take ninety minutes and asked if I was claustrophobic. Kelly immediately said, "No," so I thought, "Okay, if she doesn't think I am, I will go with that answer."

Then the doctor said, "Since you will be in there so long, maybe you could do math problems or something in your head."

I thought that was such a strange suggestion, but I thought maybe I could practice one of my presentations, then she said, "You have to keep very still, or we will have to do it again."

That ruled out the presentation. I would be too animated, swinging my arms all over the place trying to get my point across. Thirty minutes later, they came to get me for the MRI. The technician was extremely nice, so I immediately felt better. As he began to roll me into the area, I decided to do a bombardment of gratitude exercise. I began thinking how grateful I was to the person who invented the MRI allowing the doctors to get information to diagnose my symptoms. I was grateful to the people who built the machine, the people who shipped the machine, the people who maintained the machine, the people who kept the area around the machine clean, the technicians who worked the machine, the people who trained the technicians, the parents of all these people. I was so calm and felt so much gratitude that I could have stayed in there for hours!

I was so grateful that I had been prepared for this whole hospital experience because of my training and work as a Success Principle Coach. The importance and benefits of gratitude, Take 100% Responsibility for Your Life, Event + Response = Outcome, the Compassionate Mirror Ritual. As I laid in that hospital bed, I asked myself, "How do I want to show up for this experience?"

The doctor also said I needed a lumbar puncture. Those words and what I imagined the procedure to involve scared me. I told Kelly I was scared and she jumped up and started singing and doing the dance I did on December 11 at that last workshop for "Here I Stand in My Power" by Karen Drucker. Everyone started laughing and it certainly lightened the moment and made me smile.

On Friday, the doctor came in and gave me the diagnosis. It was Multiple Sclerosis after all. MS was the suspicion from the beginning, but the confirmation was like a punch in the stomach. I tried to listen carefully, but my mind began to wander as I could hardly believe what I was hearing.

Kelly and Michael were extremely supportive and appeared calm, but I knew this was rocking their worlds too. Prior to receiving the diagnosis, they had told me, "Mom, remember how you have handled and taken care of yourself with the diabetes. You have taken good care of the diabetes for forty-five years. You will do the same thing if you are diagnosed with MS, so don't be reading things and getting scared."

After everyone went home that night, I went into the bathroom and sobbed for what seemed like twenty minutes but was probably more like five, still in disbelief.

I looked in the mirror and said:

Noreen, I acknowledge you for allowing yourself to sob and feel the feelings.

Noreen, I am so proud of you for asking the question, how do you want to show up for this,

Noreen, I acknowledge you for doing the Compassionate Mirror Ritual tonight.

Noreen, I love you.

You deserve the very best.

I was released from the hospital on Christmas Eve, with both Kelly and Michael coming to pick me up. We went to my apartment to shower and pack a bag and then we were off to Kelly's apartment for the next week.

I was so grateful to be out of the hospital for Christmas Eve. I was so grateful to have two amazing, caring children who made me laugh and made me feel so loved.

At that time, I really had no idea the impact MS was going to have on my life. I expected to get full feeling back from the waist down and thought I would be back in full action in a couple of weeks. Little did I know that I wouldn't be able to drive for four months or that my daily walks would soon become a thing of the past. I would just be stuck in the house, consumed with doctor appointments, phone calls, follow-ups and gathering all the medical information. I would no longer be running my business and my energy would reach at an all-time low, that I would wonder if my life would ever be the same.

On the day I was released from the hospital, I was just grateful for my family. Kelly had the next week off from work for the holidays and had an elevator in her apartment building so that's where I would be staying. Kelly, Michael, and I celebrated Christmas Eve with my daughter-in-law Sarah, Kelly's partner Chris, and my sister Patti, along with the beloved family pets, Snickers and Ruby, of course. I was grateful to be home and around all of those whom I held so near and dear. When Kelly and Chris went to bed, their dog Snickers, who always slept in their bed, jumped up on my bed positioned herself on my lower abdomen and pelvic area and remained there with me for the entire evening. I felt her warmth and love and felt safe and grateful to be out of the hospital.

On Christmas day, Sarah and Michael, who were planning on hosting Christmas dinner at their apartment, brought everything from their apartment to cook a nice meal and have a beautiful celebration. All was well in the world, at least for now. Feeling was beginning to come back to pelvic area and feet, but my knees felt like they had thick rubber bands around them, a feeling that would last well into October.

By the end of April, even though my knees still felt like they had rubber bands around them, I told my son, who had been driving my car while I still lacked feeling in my feet, I wanted to try driving. He said, "Well, not a regular street, but we can go to a parking lot."

I started laughing, "Who is the parent here anyway?"

I agreed to go to the parking lot at the park. I hadn't driven in four months, so I figured it might be strange. I got into the driver's seat, buckled the seat belt and felt very excited to drive. I began driving and it felt very comfortable. My son started saying, "Ok, go a little faster. Ok, step on the break. Ok, turn." He said, "You are doing great, do you want to try driving home?" I was like a little kid who was just asked, "Would you like an ice cream cone?"

I said, "Yes, yes, I am so excited!"

After I successfully drove back home, we discussed, and Michael said, "Well, if Dad can drive me home, I would leave your car here."

I felt like I had gained a little control. I could drive to the park, I could go get my nails done, and I could go to the grocery store. Yay, it was a beginning.

A couple of days later, I received an email from Kripalu thanking me for volunteering to assist Megha at Introduction to Yoga and Meditation and that a reservation had been made in my name. I had assisted this program four times before, but suddenly I wondered if I would still be able to assist. I purchased a bus ticket from NYC to the Berkshires because I knew I wasn't ready to drive three hours, but I still felt a bit apprehensive. Much to my delight, I was able to take the daily walks up the driveway. I scheduled a massage for Saturday night and was able to perform all the requirements of assisting, including partnering with Megha for some demonstrations and doing the Moon Salutation.

After the program, Megha, the other assistant, Pam, and I had lunch together outside at a picnic table. Megha invited us both back to assist in October. I was absolutely thrilled and relieved, thinking that if she is inviting us back, I guess she also feels it went well.

Megha and I had a wonderful walk after lunch. I was still wrestling with what was going to be possible for me and what wasn't. I shared some of my fears and experiences from the previous four months. She listened intently, placed her hands on my knees to send healing energy and gave me a big hug. I felt supported in every inch of my body.

***

Change comes bearing gifts. New beginnings are a complete surprise, sometimes bringing devastation and disbelief. While still reeling from the MS diagnosis, I was faced with a decision: Do I resist this unexpected change, or do I explore it with curiosity and look for the blessing? Perhaps wait for the blessing to reveal itself? I have learned in the past to trust myself and my intuition. I knew I needed to trust the process. As soon as I was diagnosed, I knew this was going to be a journey like no other. I felt vulnerable, scared and uncertain. This was a very new challenge for me.

I think of 2017 as the dark year. I was in disbelief at first, I didn't drive for four months, I wasn't running my business anymore, I was no longer taking my daily four-mile walks, I barely had the energy to prepare my meals and had no interest in going anywhere. I was in very unfamiliar territory and felt completely lost. One thing I did have was music. Music has always been such a big part of my life, sometimes lifting me up, sometimes calming me down. George Eliot once said, "I think I should have no other mortal wants, if I could always have plenty of music. It seems to infuse strength into my limbs and ideas into my brain. Life seems to go on without effort when I am filled with music."

I listened almost exclusively to Karen Drucker and the positive messages in her songs. I needed it to lift my spirits. Her music took on a much deeper meaning for me. In the morning, I would play her songs on shuffle and it seemed as though just the right songs played at just the right time. "I Will Be Gentle With Myself" would play and I would be gentle with myself, then "Let It Be Easy" would come on and I would think, yes, just let it be easy. Then I would hear the first two notes of "I Wish For You", a song I used leading Let Your Yoga Dance, and I would leap to me feet and dance through the room doing the movements I had created and just for a few minutes I felt like my old self! It was these little sparkles that kept me going. My legs were compromised and my energy diminished, but my spirit was fully alive.

When Karen heard I had been diagnosed with MS, she called me at home. As we were talking, she asked, "Is that me in the background?"

I said, "Yes, I have Karen Drucker on the iPod and Karen Drucker on the phone," as we both laughed. It was so sweet of her to call and so unexpected.

After that, Karen and I stayed in touch via email. I shared my gratitude for what was making a very big difference in my life. Karen's particular style and message was just what I needed. She was always so kind with her responses and even said I was inspiring her while she was working on her newest CD, which made my day.

At the end of April, I began taking a weekly injection to hopefully stop or at least slow the progression of the disease. The day the medication was delivered, I had a complete meltdown. I was alone in my apartment and began to sob viscerally.

For the first four weeks, I had to use a syringe. I would set it in a device so that the first week I received ¼ dose, the second week ½ dose, the third week ¾ dose, and the last week a full dose. After that, I could use a pen for the weekly injection.

When I was diagnosed with Type 1 Diabetes at age fourteen, the syringe was very small and only had to go right under the skin. The syringe for the MS medication was much larger because it had to go into the muscle.

The first night I had to do the injection a sweet nurse named Maggie came to my apartment to teach me and my daughter came for moral support. I panicked and kept saying I was scared and couldn't do it. Finally, I said to Maggie that when I was younger, I did it slow. She said, "Ok, do it slow."

So, I stretched the skin with the index finger and thumb of one hand and I placed the syringe on the skin with the other hand and began to gently push. It pierced the skin, and did not hurt so I kept pushing until what I imagined to be a four to five-inch needle was all the way in. I injected the medication, removed the needle and breathed a big sigh of relief. Maggie said, "You did great!"

Kelly said, "Wow, I never saw you that scared, Mama."

The following week I measured the syringe and it was only three inches. Perception is not always reality. For some reason, I was feeling exceptionally scared about the injection and remembering how scared I was when I was fourteen and told I would have to take injections the rest of my life. I had always been afraid of needles. I was also thinking about when I was a little girl going to the neighborhood doctor, Dr. Cohen, and I had my arms wrapped around my Mom's waist. I felt like I was revisiting all those earlier scary experiences and thinking, "I cannot believe this is all happening again."

When I mentioned the story about holding my mom's waist to my sister, Patti, she said, "I remember one time when they all had to hold you down--the nurse, the doctor, and Mom--you were so scared."

The memories are in our tissues, and this was clearly a profound experience for me.

The doctor advised me that I should do the injections in the evening because I would have flu-like symptoms. She instructed me to take a pain reliever before the injection and then another one right before bed.

For the first few weeks, I would wake up during the night shivering and feeling feverish. My eyes had a little burning sensation and I would wake up in the morning with a headache. Once I took the pain reliever in the morning, however, all symptoms would disappear.

Through trial and error, the doctor and I came up with a good plan. I took one pain reliever an hour before the injection, two pain relievers two hours after the injection, and one pain reliever at bedtime. It worked! No flu-like symptoms, I felt so relieved.

During this time, I tried to reflect on the positives. My son, Michael, and I were in the process of writing my book, something I had wanted to do for twenty years, if not longer, but it was only after the diagnosis made me slow down that I actually had the time to sit and focus on the hard mental work of actually writing the book. My former husband, Mike, was driving me everywhere I needed to go from January through April, Kelly and Michael were driving me to my appointments with the MS Specialist. The four of us were spending more time together than we had since before they went off to college. How could I not at least see the blessing in that?

I slowly began to adjust to the weekly injections and move forward one small glorious step at a time.

My legs never fully regained their feeling. My knees felt like that had thick rubber bands around them and my legs from the knees to the ankles always felt a bit tingling and had different degrees of tightness. I was never sure what affected the tightness. Sometimes it was very noticeable and sometimes it was hardly noticeable. This was very new territory for me.

It was becoming quite a lesson in vulnerability, patience and receiving. My legs were compromised and my energy diminished. All my decisions were based on my health first. I didn't have the energy to do much and I didn't really care.

***

That first summer following the diagnosis was very unusual because I never felt like going to the beach. Never mind wanting to walk on the boardwalk I didn't even feel like sitting on a bench at the boardwalk. I always felt tired and didn't feel like it was worth it. I had become quite the couch potato.

One afternoon in mid-August, I opened Facebook and the first post was Karen Drucker and Joan Borysenko sitting in front of a statue of Shiva (goddess of transformation) at Kripalu, one of my favorite places. They were doing a weekend retreat at Kripalu. I got this surge of excitement during a time when I hadn't really felt excited about anything.

I asked myself the familiar question of "What do you want? Is it worth it?" I wanted to experience this retreat and decided that it would be worth it to attempt the longest drive since I had felt that pins and needles tingling the previous December. This would be a real test, but I thought I could take two pain relievers at the beginning and if my leg started to hurt, I would stop along the way and take a break. I made arrangements to stay locally on Friday and Saturday night. This way, I could take my time on the ride up and the ride home. My daughter was concerned and purchased a cushion for my car, which did make it more comfortable. I contacted Karen to tell her I'd be coming for the day Saturday and we made plans to have lunch together. I felt so excited that I made appointments for a haircut, manicure and pedicure. Even just those little treats of self-care started to make me feel better.

A few days later, Karen emailed me to ask if I would like to do a reading on the theme of GRATITUDE at her chanting evening during the retreat at Kripalu. My eyes filled with tears as I read her request. I was so grateful to Karen for not only her music but also her kindness. I felt so honored to do a reading.

When I entered the Main Hall on the night of the Chanting Evening, I was welcomed by the glow of the gorgeous purple and blue lighting that highlighted the stage where Karen would be performing. I felt honored as I delivered the following reading I had chosen by poet Patience Strong:

I am thankful for everything God bestows

I am thankful for the for the joys and sorrows, for the blessings and the blows.

I am thankful for the wisdom gained through hardships and adversity.

I am thankful for the undertones as well as the melody.

I am thankful for the benefits both great and small-

And never fail in gratitude for the divinest gift of all:

the love of friends that I have known in times of failure and success.

O may the first prayer of the day be always one of thankfulness.

Listening to Karen perform live totally soothed my soul and lifted my spirits. I had a good night's rest and felt elevated the entire ride home. I stopped to see my daughter-in-law, Sarah, for her birthday on the way home and had so much fun visiting with her. As I continued driving home after our visit, I realized I had turned a corner. Something felt different; something felt better.

***

Since the diagnosis, my sister, Patti, with whom I have always been close, became even closer as we began staying in touch daily. When we're together, Patti and I have always laughed so hard that we almost wet our pants. That laughter made a big difference during that first year. Towards the end of the summer, we visited the beach house our grandparents used to own where we grew up and made so many special memories.

As we pulled down Maple Lane, I spotted my favorite tree from when we grew up. My grandparents had waterfront property on Peconic Bay and also a lot along Maple Lane where we used to play and where the tree still stood. It looked as big and beautiful as ever, full of so many memories of our childhood. We climbed that tree and had a swing on one of the branches of the tree. One time, we had a carnival with our cousins around the tree. We put up a tent by the tree and my sister Kathy sat inside and pretended to be a fortune teller.

As we drove past, I told Patti to stop so I could take a photo of our tree. As I was snapping away, Patti said, "There is a man sitting on the porch over there."

I said, "Oh, should I say something?"

Without really thinking about it, I stepped out of the car and approached the house, explaining to the man sitting on the porch that my grandfather sold Jim and Helen Dooley this property and I just wanted to get a photo of our special tree. I asked if he was any relationship to Helen and Jim Dooley. He stood up and said, "I am not related, but Eileen is."

He walked me into the backyard and said, "Eileen, I have a visitor here for you."

She said, "Let me come closer."

I said, "Oh, you won't recognize me, but I am John Scully's granddaughter."

She replied that she was close to my cousin, Jack, who had passed away. She reminded me so much of her mother, Helen. She looked like her and had her mannerisms and kindness. She and I talked for a little while and then I said, "Please come out and meet my sister, Patti."

Eileen caught us up on all the neighborhood news as we reminisced and swapped stories from years long since passed. We shared memories of Nana's beautiful pink rose bushes and how Nana would always ring the bell for dinner. I shared the story my grandfather told me just after I had been diagnosed with Diabetes about how her father Jim would swim back and forth and how he didn't have to take insulin because of his swimming.

It was a very special day. She walked us down to the beach and even brought us water bottles later in the afternoon. She made us feel so welcomed. In recent years, we had often felt like strangers when we visited, but she welcomed us so warmly that we felt like family.

We left in the late afternoon and stopped at a supermarket to get some shrimp cocktail to eat in the car. I looked at the smaller shrimp and said, "Okay, let's get a pound to share."

Patti said, "Let's get the jumbo shrimp!"

Those did look awesome, so I agreed, and we purchased some cocktail sauce, the jumbo shrimp, and some seltzer. The clerk at the fish counter was even nice enough to give us a plastic container for us to use as a dish. Off we went to enjoy our little picnic. The shrimp was delicious, the perfect ending to our beautiful day. For the rest of the ride home, I kept saying, "ALWAYS CHOOSE THE JUMBO SHRIMP." A great life lesson indeed.

***

In October 2017, I flew to California to attend Karen Drucker's retreat, *The Call of Something More*, so I could thank her for all her support over the past year. Her kindness through phone calls and emails and listening to her positive music soothed my soul and lifted my spirits continuously. I received so much at this retreat. First, there was a wonderful gathering of loving women, Karen's music and singing, the calming vastness of the ocean and a few deer who were guarding and guiding our meeting room. such an exceptional experience. Joy and Bliss met Love and Healing.

Karen asked the attendees what we would like to release while we were there? I wanted to release my "scary" MS fears. Then she asked what we wanted to plant. If I released my scary MS fears, I wanted to plant HOPE. She invited us to symbolically throw a stone with what we wanted to release in the ocean the next day. I walked into the ocean until the water was up to my knees and as I looked down, I saw an oblong stone about four inches in diameter sitting there all by itself. I knew it was my rock of HOPE to take home with me. I threw my stone of scary fears and picked up my rock of HOPE, rinsed it in the water and placed it safely in my top pocket of my blouse.

On the plane ride home, I realized I had never truly felt hopeless in my life. Not even after my father's death, when it would have been so easy to give in to the fear and succumb to hopelessness. I have faced countless challenges and had to overcome immense pain and great fear, but I had never felt hopeless. I realized that although I had not been hopeless during the previous year, I had lost some hope. I reflected on the rock I was bringing back with me to be my anchor and thought about the beautiful butterfly mug I purchased from the Asilomar gift shop with the following words printed:

Advice from a BUTTERFLY

Get out of your cocoon

Take yourself lightly

Look for the sweetness in life

Take time to smell the flowers

Catch a breeze

Treat yourself like a monarch

Let your true colors show!

When I returned to New York, my new favorite morning coffee mug served as an anchor to remind me of releasing fear, planting hope and sharing my gratitude with Karen.

***

As the 2017 holiday season approached, I began to feel more optimistic as I adjusted to the new norm. I started to think about my annual Win List, knowing that this year, it would be a bit different. My Wins were about overcoming obstacles. I started to think I had so many triumphs. On December 30, I began to write my list. As usual, the more I wrote, the more motivated I felt. By the time I finished, I was inspired to create a goal list for 2018 as well. Because I had been so preoccupied with the MS diagnosis, the year before was the first one since I began creating Win Lists that I didn't have a goal list on January 1st. Here I was less than one year later, feeling more like myself again.

As I looked forward and set some goals for 2018, I became so excited and motivated, I even explored an Ayurveda program I wanted to take at Kripalu and found myself submitting an application. It wasn't even lunchtime yet on December 30, 2017, and I had already cooked and eaten breakfast, completed my Win List for 2017, set goals for 2018, and applied for the Ayurveda program at Kripalu (which I then completed - now on my 2018 Wins List!). Creating Wins Lists helps shift energy in a positive direction. It is so easy for us to forget all our amazing accomplishments and victories. Once we start writing them down, they become more real.

***

In February 2018, I attended Posi Festival in Tampa, Florida. There was a faith lift each morning, presentations by keynote speakers, lunch served at poolside, daily workshops, and concerts every night, Thursday through Sunday. Four days of beautiful music, fabulous company and warm temperatures. Sign me up! I went to a flute class because I have always been fascinated with flutes but never played one. Towards the end of the workshop as we held flutes and were taught some basic techniques, the instructor said, "Trick your brain into thinking you are young, do something new."

I thought, "Yes! I have not done anything new for some time," and purchased the flute I had been using in the class, made of cedar wood adorned with turquoise gems and a small wooden bird perched on top. At another workshop on drumming, a fabulous singer named Deirdre invited me to dance. I did not give it a second thought. I jumped up and started dancing. I was not thinking of my legs, my balance or my ability. I was totally in my body. I danced and danced until my shirt was full of perspiration. It felt great, I had not danced like that since my last workshop in December 2016. I met new friends, enjoyed lunch poolside and dinner out every night. I took a chance, showed up, and had no idea what to expect but was so happy I did. I came back filled up and feeling better than I had in fourteen months.

After I returned, I realized I was turning 60 in six months and made the decision to look forward to my birthday rather than dread it. I themed the birthday celebration, "60 and Sparkling!"

The festivities began with a beautiful dinner in Manhattan with my sister, Patti; my children, Kelly and Michael; their partners, Chris and Sarah; and my friend, Karen Drucker. Then I headed to Albany for a Nia class (dancing and yoga) where my friend Karen was singing, then to Kripalu where Megha and I assisted Karen Drucker. My cousin Helen and some friends from Let Your Yoga Dance attended the weekend. We sang, we danced, we laughed, and we cried it was an exceptional weekend.

On the day of my birthday, my daughter had a dinner party at her apartment where she gave me a Happy Birthday book with letters and photos from family, friends and colleagues. I cried as I read the thoughtful letters on every page. What a wonderful gift Kelly made for me! I will treasure it always. The weekend after my birthday, I went to lunch with my children, their partners and my former husband. Michael prepared a playlist of 60 songs to continue the theme of "60 and Sparkling." What a treat!

In October, I went back to Asilomar for another retreat with Karen Drucker. I felt so much better, so much stronger than last year when I attended. Dancing on the beach, yoga on the beach, Karen singing and creating an amazing sacred space. It lifted my spirits, soothed my soul and healed my heart. I left Asilomar with abundant joy and peace of mind.

From there it was on to San Francisco for the final adventure of "60 and Sparkling!" and to mark one more item off my list of lifetime goals: to walk across the Golden Gate Bridge. Karen and her husband, John, joined me as the sun shined in the beautiful, clear blue sky of a perfect 60-degree day (even the weather was 60 and Sparkling!), and all was right in the world. As we walked from the San Francisco side, up to the left were mountains all around us. Karen and John were sharing stories about the bridge and the area, Alcatraz off to the right. The deep blue water looked so big and vast to me and everything felt so spacious as we walked and talked, enjoying the breeze and witnessing the sun beginning to set as we came back across.

Walking across the Golden Gate Bridge was something I always wanted to do, but after the MS diagnosis, I was not sure I was going to be able to do it. When the time came, my body memory took over and everything felt effortless, the weather, the company, it was like I was floating across the bridge. I was feeling stronger one small glorious step at a time and I knew I was going to be able to do it. Karen walking with me made it even more special and significant because I felt she had been so supportive since the diagnosis. The word that sprang to mind that day and continues to be my feeling of that day is SPECTACULAR. Karen took a great photo of me with my arms extended in the air, which I then made the screensaver on my phone and printed as an 8x10 photo for my living room. Just looking at that photo fuels my spirit and lights me up. I feel the JOY.

I am so blessed, I am so grateful!

***

Multiple Sclerosis slowed me down, forced me to pay attention to my health and energy first, caused me to ask for help more often, be more patient, be more present, and savor every precious moment. A blessing in disguise.

As unsettling, scary, and challenging as 2017 was, 2018 was full of growth, unexpected pleasures, grounding, expanded awareness and gratitude. I became extremely aware of what I want, need and deserve. My priorities crystallized around my health, my kids and my bliss.

Challenges and pain are inevitable but suffering and remaining stuck is a choice.

Our response to the challenges and pain is our point of power. Feel the pain, allow it to pass through, but do not invite it to stay.

Challenges come bearing blessings. Be patient and the blessings will reveal themselves.

Choose JOY. Choose LOVE. If you want to truly Live in Joy, you must allow the tears to turn into pearls of wisdom and the pain to give way to unconditional love, one small glorious step at a time.

Choose Joy

For more information:
Noreen Kelty can be contacted at Noreenkelty@gmail.com

Jack Canfield's events and trainings:
www.JackCanfield.com

Karen Drucker's music and events:
www.KarenDrucker.com

Tama Kieves's events:
www.TamaKieves.com

Megha Nancy Buttenheim and Let Your Yoga Dance:
www.LetYourYogaDance.com